# Tanya B. Ditto

# Dalmatians

Everything About Purchase, Care,
Nutrition, Breeding, Behavior, and Training

With Color Photographs by Well-Known Photographers
and Drawings by Michele Earle-Bridges

Consulting Editor: Matthew M. Vriends, Ph.D.

BARRON'S

**Photo Credits:** Jane Donahue (Moments by Jane/ Wellesley, Massachusetts): Inside front cover. Michele Earle-Bridges: Front cover; pages 27; 28; 45; 46 bottom left; back cover top right, bottom left. Gary Ellis: Pages 9 bottom; 10. Dick Hamer: Pages 63; 64; back cover top left, bottom right. Robert Lauwer: Page 46 top right. Wim van Vught: Page 9 top; inside back cover.

**About the Author:**

Tanya B. Ditto, a former high school English teacher, lives on Little Lake Farms, a 70-acre waterfowl refuge nestled deep in south Mississippi's piney woods. She and her husband, Bill, raise Labrador retrievers and ornamental waterfowl, including Royal mute and Australian swans, and they host a popular bed-and-breakfast. A freelance writer, a member of the Dog Writers' Association of America, the Dalmatian Club of Greater Atlanta, and Hub City Dog Fanciers, Tanya, in her spare time, works with Moppity Dot on obedience training.

**Advice and Warning:** This book is concerned with buying, keeping, and raising dalmatians. The publisher and the author think it is important to point out that the advice and information for dalmatian maintenance applies to healthy, normally developed animals. Anyone who buys an adult dalmatian or one from an animal shelter must consider that the animal may have behavioral problems and may, for example, bite without any visible provocation. Such anxiety-biters are dangerous for the owner as well as for the general public.

Caution is further advised in the association of children with a dalmatian, in meetings with other dogs, and in exercising the dog without a leash.

© Copyright 1991 by Barron's Educational Series, Inc.

*All inquiries should be addressed to:*
Barron's Educational Series, Inc.
250 Wireless Boulevard
Hauppauge, NY 11788

International Standard Book No. 0-8120-4605-6

Library of Congress Catalog Card No. 91-4778

**Library of Congress Cataloging-in-Publication Data**

Ditto, Tanya B.
    Dalmatians : a complete pet owner's manual / Tanya B. Ditto; consulting editor, Matthew M. Vriends.
        p.      cm.
    ISBN 0-8120-4605-6
    1. Dalmatian dog.      I. Vriends, Matthew M.,
1937–          . II. Title.
SF429.D3D57   1991
636.7'2—dc20                                  91-4778
                                                  CIP

PRINTED IN HONG KONG

234      4900      98765432

# Contents

# *Preface*

You probably can think of 101 reasons why dalmatians are popular. For one thing, these gentle spotted dogs are easy to train. They are courteous and well mannered. They certainly are decorated uniquely.

The breed has a rich and complex history. It roamed the continent of Europe with nomadic Gypsy bands and decorated the carriages of aristocratic England. It is the world's only coach dog.

In the early days of the twentieth century, the breed's numbers declined. Today, however, the dal is regaining its old popularity. In 1989, the number of dalmatians registered with the American Kennel Club jumped up seven notches. In 1990, it was listed as the AKC's twenty-fourth most popular dog. Signs are that the rise will continue.

Dalmatian owners are pleased that their breed is getting recognition. Longtime owners, however, also recognize that a sudden jump in a breed's popularity can be cause for worry. Historically, when too high a demand is placed on breeders, an "any-dog-will-do" panic kicks in.

Dr. Eleanor Frankling, a well-known dalmatian breeder, judge, and author, once commented, "The breed has become popular—the last thing that a dedicated dalmatian lover would want."

Hasty and unscrupulous breeding brings with it two worst case fears. The first is the real possibility of overproduction. A surplus of pups could be produced for which there would not be enough demand. Unwanted animals could be destined for animal care shelters. Not a pleasant thought.

In addition, in their haste to produce litters, thoughtless breeders can downgrade the quality of a dalmatian. Faults long hidden could surface. Yes, the breed does have a few, very few, ongoing concerns that you as a prospective owner should know about. These concerns are given full consideration in the section on Hereditary Problems (page 11).

Do you know why you chose a dalmatian? Do you know what it means when a judge says of a dog, "Its conformation is excellent"? Did you know that the dalmatian has a reputation for having a quick memory? Did you ever hear it called the "gentleman from Dalmatia"? Have you ever heard the dal referred to as the only true coach dog in the world and wonder why? In this book, you'll learn the answers to these questions and more.

This manual is written to help those who admire the dalmatian to make a decision about ownership. The text highlights the responsibilities of owning a dal, and tracks the dalmatian from puppy through old age. The chapters present, in layman's terms, information on feeding, training, health care, and specific behavior problems.

It is written for Meghan, Anna, Crystie, Christopher, and Kelsey who are degree candidates in the school of puppy socialization.

I would like to acknowledge the support of my husband, Bill, who cheerfully designed kennels and constructed whelping boxes, and weighed, dewormed, and nail clipped numerous litters. He cleaned and sanitized countless runs and lugged home multitudinous 40-pound sacks of kibble. He more than once served as a midwife, especially when two beautiful females, within hours of each other, presented us with 18 pups.

My deep appreciation to Rosalind and Charles Gunn for being good neighbors to all God's creatures, and to Dr. Matthew Vriends for offering friendship and encouragement.

Dr. Tom Ricks, D.V.M., read and improved the chapter on injuries, first aid, and illness. All of us—Sandy, Molly, Bully, Dotty, Bill, and I—thank him for his assistance.

I would like to especially thank the many breeders who responded to questionnaires and telephone calls with enthusiasm and specific hints. Thanks to the Dalmatian Club of America for providing up-to-date literature. In particular, I would like to acknowledge Eleanor Andry and her Reno video, and technicians Trish Powell, Tammy Eaton, Bobbye Moore, and Margaret Simpson for their unflagging enthusiasm. Thanks to Trish Lambert and the members of the Hub City Dog Fanciers for training assistance, and certainly to Betty Loflin for producing the dalmatian who plays the starring role in our lives, Ma Petite Dotty.

Tanya B. Ditto

# History of the Dalmatian

## Origins and Early History

Is today's dalmatian descended from the famous tiger dog of ancient legend? Is this the same breed once owned exclusively by a Mohammedan princess? Or is the dal simply a smaller version of the Great Dane?

A re-reading of old guidebooks reveals much of invention, little of fact. Some writers of yesterday's guides probably never had seen a dalmatian. Other authors read what was available at the time and seized as truth amazingly odd bits of information.

Some authoritative writers refuted conclusions drawn by earlier authors. All of this energy resulted in imaginative speculation. Did the dalmatian reach Italy in the company of the camp followers trailing behind Caesar's conquering legions?

For that matter, is the dal part Gypsy? Could it have traveled to Europe during hundreds of years of massive tribal migrations?

The dalmatian's birthplace, variously reported as India, Denmark, France, and Austria, may never be known. Engravings centuries old depict spotted dogs following horse-drawn wheeled carts. Researchers found early references to spotted dogs in writings of the Greeks and Romans. It was left to the middle eighteenth century authors to refer to the spotted dog by name: dalmatian.

Could the breed have originated in Dalmatia, a province of present-day Yugoslavia? Today's historians have agreed to disagree.

Let us, also, leave it at that. The dalmatian is a truly historic breed, its origin as spattered as its spots.

## The Traditional Dalmatian

If the dalmatian's place of birth is shrouded in the mists of history, its abilities are equally well highlighted. Always a close companion of man, the first publicly noted use of the dalmatian was as a hunting dog. The dal's keen nose and resemblance to the pointer led hunters to field train it. In fact, it was as a hunting dog that the dalmatian was brought to England.

Many dalmatians prove themselves the retrieving equals of Labradors, setters, and spaniels. At three months of age, our dalmatian stopped and held up one front foot when a stray odor or movement caught her attention. At four months, she routinely outraced her kennelmate, a seven-month-old Labrador retriever, to the disk or stick or whatever we threw for them to retrieve. (In those days she stood on the disk instead of returning it. This was not a fault—the second dog was twice her size.)

Today, the American Kennel Club does not classify the dalmatian as a sporting dog, but rather as one of the 12-member nonsporting group, which includes Boston terriers, chow chows, poodles, Lhasa apsos, and keeshonds.

## What's In a Name?

A dalmatian has many nicknames, some related to its responsibilities, some to its coloration. The dal has been known as the plum pudding dog, the firehouse dog, the spotted dick, the spotted dog of Dalmatia and the carriage dog. Among its most ancient and honorable titles is the designation of coach dog.

## Coach Dogs

In Europe, the dalmatian had for centuries slept in the stables as companions to the horses. Coach dogs, as they were called, arrived in America with the early settlers. Still, the breed was not commonly known until the late 1800s. Historians, citing references to coach dogs in George Washington's correspondence, tell us that he owned at least one dalmatian.

The breed was well established in England by the early nineteenth century where the combination of the dalmatian's affinity for horses and its decorative spots brought it to the attention of the wealthy. When the "four-in-hand" coach became a

# History of the Dalmatian

fashionable mode of travel, the spotted dog running behind the trap, or under it, was much in demand. Valued as a deterrent to highwaymen during the day, the dog followed the horses to the stables at night, again standing guard over its master's belongings.

In the early stages of training, the dalmatian worked behind a two-wheel cart. An already-trained dal was put in the lead. Often the young dog's mother rode in the cart. The puppy naturally followed. Eventually, the young dal learned to pace with the horses, running for many miles underneath the front axle of the trap, close to the horses' heels. A shy dog, or one too timid to stay in position, was a major disappointment. Only the adventurous were accepted into the breeding program.

This decorative function disappeared with the invention of the motor car. The once useful dalmatian coach dog lost popularity with the public. For several years, regional clubs continued to hold road trials, which allowed coaching training to continue. Eventually, though, even these gave way to the life-style of a new generation.

Recently, however, The Puget Sound Dalmatian Club in Washington state hosted the first American road trial in 40 years. Designed to showcase the dal's obedience and speed, two courses were set up of 12.5 (20 km) and 25 miles (40 km). The 12.5 mile course was to be run in three and one-half hours and the 25 mile course in six and one-half hours.

Points were awarded for the proper handling of a distracting hiker and dog, for proper recall, and for a long sit/down. In addition, each dog was required to pass three veterinary checkups, at the start, midway, and conclusion of the run.

Thirteen dalmatians participated in the courses. Nine passed the tests. "Road trials are the best thing that's happened to dals since spots," one happy competitor reported. Whether or not road trials for dals become popular, it is clear that the participants considered them a great success.

## Firehouse Dogs

In Great Britain and later in America, the dalmatian moved into the firehouses with the horse-drawn fire wagons. The dogs were welcomed as useful companions for the firemen and the horses.

The dalmatians learned to line up for roll call. Little fire hats adorned the collars of the best behaved. When the alarm bells rang, the trained dals led the fire engine pumper out of the station, running ahead to clear the cross streets. Once on duty, Smoky and Sparky and their kin remained at the fire scene until the crew returned.

Visitors were welcome at the neighborhood stations. Newspaper stories told of children stopping in on Saturday with lumps of sugar, apples, and candy for the horses and the dogs.

By the early 1900s, though, with the widespread adoption of the gasoline engine, the fire units were mechanized and the dalmatian was out of work again. Today many fire companies retain this traditional mascot only in poster form. The pretty, spotted head, still on guard, peers out at visitors from behind its glass wall.

## War Dogs

Some firehouse mascots got a second opportunity for service during World War II when they were drilled in rescue work. In Boston, fire department dalmatians were taught to carry messages and Red Cross supply kits, to guard property, and to search for victims, especially those buried under debris.

Learning such varied responsibilities as to refuse food from strangers, to retrieve on scent, and to climb ladders during rescue missions, Nedo, Sussex, Checkers, and Bingo Bango felt useful again.

## Show Dogs

In the late 1930s and early 1940s several country living magazines featured regular dog columnists. Kennel advertisements framed the articles.

Today, by borrowing back issues from the library, lucky readers often can find surprisingly good photographs of champions in the pedigrees of their very own pet dalmatian.

By 1936, dalmatians from Mrs. L.W. Bonney's Tally-Ho Kennels on Long Island, New York were perennial champions. Mrs. Bonney, soon to be known as "Mrs. Dalmatian," advised, "We have several litters of puppies of this old and reliable breed from which you can select specimens sound in type and quality." The kennel ad featured a photograph of three-time national specialty winner, Ch. Tally Ho Last of Sunstar.

Reigate Kennels in Smithfield, Virginia, advertised "Distinctive Dalmatians" in a 1938 *House and Garden*. In another issue, Oread Kennels of Lawrence, Kansas featured two perky dals peeking out of a laundry basket. The overhead legend announced a truth that dalmatian lovers have known for years, "The one dog that seems to fit well in any fine home."

## Circus Performers

The dalmatian's obvious joy of living makes it a natural crowd pleaser. In the circus world, dalmatians are recognized as quick, even-tempered learners. It works well with the horses and is easy to travel with. During show time, much to the crowd's delight, the dal usually plays the part of clown. With instinctive athletic balance, a circus-trained dal will roll barrels, climb tall ladders, walk tightropes, and jump broom handles.

## Disney's Dalmatians

In 1956, the antics of the puppies in Dodie Smith's book, *One Hundred and One Dalmatians,* enchanted children everywhere. Then, in 1961, cartoonists at Hollywood's Walt Disney Studios gave the spotted puppies a new image. The lovable Pongo and Perdy came to life on the big screen. It was at this magical moment that the fortune of the handsome dalmatian began to rise again.

# *Understanding Your Dalmatian*

## A Quick Look at the Dalmatian

Pointers have spots. Terriers have a short coat. Greyhounds can run. But a dalmatian will not be mistaken for any other dog.

Have you ever watched an adult dalmatian run free across a field? At full stride, a dalmatian's spine arches almost into a hoop. Its hind legs overtake and pass its forelegs.

Have you ever thrown a ball for it to retrieve — again and again and again? A full-grown dalmatian, bred to run for hours under the axle of a four-in-hand, is difficult to tire.

Ever stroked that sleek and glossy coat, unique in dogdom?

All dalmatian owners should be familiar with the American Kennel Club standard for the breed. This standard is found in Characteristics of the Breed (see page 71 ). Following, however, are some of the dal's outstanding characteristics.

## Temperament

Temperament varies in dalmatians as it does in other breeds. The dalmatian usually is good with children and makes a fine family pet. It is anxious to please, an intelligent, people-oriented breed. There is very little difference in temperament between male and female dalmatians.

An extrovert, the dalmatian is active and will wander far from home unless restrained. It is very important to have a fenced-in yard for your pet. Although assumed to be streetwise because of its heritage, no dalmatian ancestor had to face today's traffic. To have to confine this magnificent dog to a life on a leash is unfair.

The dalmatian is noted for its "smarl," a combination of smile and snarl. Tight lips are drawn back over the front teeth in a strange and occasionally disconcerting smile.

Our dal, like her friends our Labs, brings us a "present" when she comes. When called, she often will slow down just long enough to scoop up the nearest stick, pine cone, or fallen leaf before resuming her hurtle in our direction. She never stops wagging that wonderful "saber" tail.

## Pet Personality Test

Some psychologists have devised testing programs that can help determine a puppy's future disposition. This procedure is called personality testing. If you are looking for a show dog, for instance, you might want to check the puppy for confidence, one not afraid of strange sights and sounds. On the other hand, if the puppy is to be the companion of an elderly couple, one with a lower energy level might be what you will want.

The test involves taking a quick look at three aspects of a puppy's behavior: temperament, sociability, and intelligence.

William Campbell developed a very practical Puppy Behavior Test. Designed to match a puppy to the best-suited home, the test evaluates the following five behavioral tendencies.

### Can You Call the Puppy to You?

This test will give you an idea of the puppy's personality. Is it outgoing or is it shy? Step away from the puppy and try to attract it to you. See how willingly it comes, how quickly it comes, or whether it comes at all.

### Will the Puppy Follow if You Walk Away?

Stand next to the puppy. Now turn and walk in the opposite direction. (Be sure it sees you do this.) Whether the puppy follows you, stays still, or walks the other way can be a test of its independence.

Dalmation puppies are born pure white. Dense black or ▶ liver-brown spots begin to come in at about two weeks.

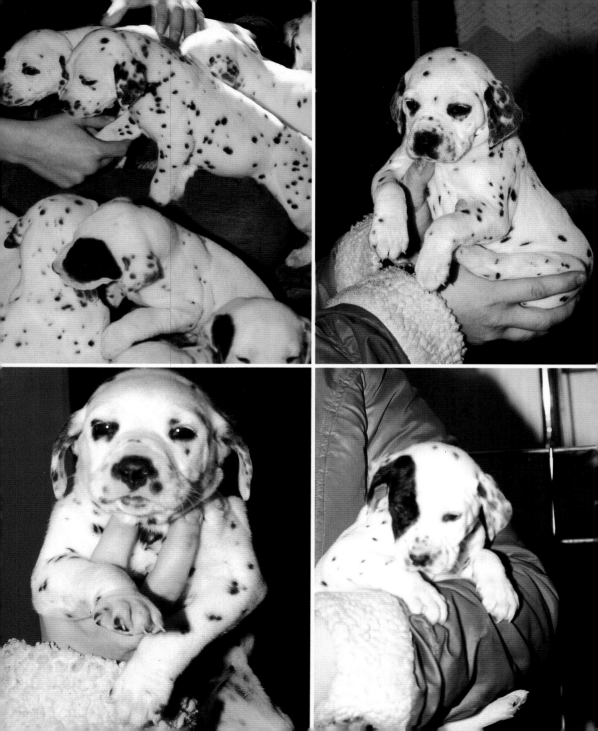

# *Understanding Your Dalmatian*

## How Active Is the Puppy?

Gently roll the puppy onto its back. With one hand on its chest, hold it down for about 30 seconds. How does the puppy respond? Does it ever settle down?

## Can You Calm Down the Puppy?

Gently stroke the puppy from head to tail. Do this several times until you get a clear reaction, which will range from submission to biting or growling.

## Will the Puppy Accept Physical Restraint?

Putting both hands around the puppy's belly, lift it off the ground. How permissive is the puppy to this situation? How much does it struggle and for how long?

Match your own score to the results of this quiz with your answers to the next chapter's life-style preference questions (see Consider Your Life-style, page 16). Add in your emotions: "He was the cutest one in the litter. When I saw him, I had to have him." That puppy is waiting for you.

## Coat Colors

A dalmatian is born pure white. Dense black or liver-brown spots begin to come in at about two weeks. The spots are round and well defined. Although litters of black and white and liver brown and white dogs are common, it is not proper for one dog to have a coating containing both colors. "Patches," which are appreciably larger colored areas present at birth, are unacceptable in the breed.

◀ While handling a puppy you can determine how active it is, whether or not it will calm down easily, and whether or not it will accept physical restraint. Puppies with patches may be adorable, but should never be bred (see page 68).

The dalmatian's nose should be the same color as its spots.

## Measurements

An eight-week-old dalmatian puppy is "almost square" from withers to rump and rump to ground. Its feet are round and its toes are arched. Its eyes are round, the darker the better.

A full-grown dalmatian is a lean, medium-size dog, about knee-high to an adult. Usually 19 to 24 inches (48–61 cm) at the shoulder, its adult weight will range from 45 to 70 pounds (20–32 kg).

## Hardiness

The dalmatian possesses a fabled endurance. Its history of running for hours on end, keeping pace behind or under a horse-drawn carriage, speaks well for its stamina. The dalmatian's deep chest, which allows plenty of heartroom and space for lung expansion, prevents it from becoming winded.

Normally hardy and healthy, dalmatians can live to the great old age of sixteen or seventeen years. The average, mostly trouble-free, life span of your new friend is between eleven and thirteen years.

## Hereditary Problems in the Dalmatian

The dal has two primary and somewhat unique hereditary tendencies. The dalmatian is one of several breeds subject to hereditary deafness. It is the only breed whose liver cannot metabolize uric acid correctly. The dal's deaf gene and its uric acid transport system have been the subject of numerous studies.

### The Deaf Gene

The breeds that have a problem with hereditary deafness often have a white or predominantly

# *Understanding Your Dalmatian*

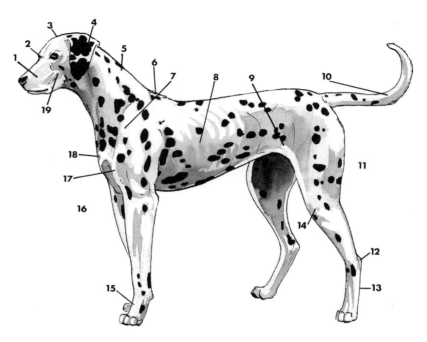

An overall look at the dalmatian:

| | | | |
|---|---|---|---|
| 1. muzzle | 6. withers | 11. hindquarters | 16. forequarters |
| 2. stop | 7. shoulder | 12. hock | 17. brisket |
| 3. skull | 8. rib cage | 13. rear pastern | 18. chest |
| 4. ear | 9. loin | 14. stifle | 19. cheek |
| 5. neckline | 10. saber tail | 15. front pastern | |

white coat. Sealyhams, Border collies, and terriers are among those breeds afflicted.

**How To Check for Deafness:** These common home tests are subjective and consequently subject to interpretation.

Observe the puppy with others of the litter. The ear flaps of a deaf dog will not be as active as its littermates. Take the puppy away from the litter and set it down. Wait until the puppy is not looking at you. Shout and clap your hands. Rattle a spoon in a food bowl. Slam a door. Blow a whistle, if possible, in various pitches. Don't stamp on the floor if there is any possibility of a vibration. See if your veterinarian has any suggestions.

Conscientious breeders check their puppies at about four weeks, at six weeks, and before they are sold. Deaf dogs usually are put down. Do not purchase a deaf puppy. A deaf dalmatian will be fearful, occasionally neurotic, often snappish, and a danger to itself and others.

# Understanding Your Dalmatian

## Uric Acid Transport System

Although other breeds are susceptible to bladder stones, the dalmatian is the only breed that has a genetic reason for them. Because of its system's inability to break down food proteins, the dalmatian has a tendency to form uric acid bladder stones. These stones, usually appearing when the dog is two to ten years old, can be painful and life threatening.

Some of the contributing factors to stone formatian are too much protein in the diet, high levels of minerals, lack of regular exercise, and infrequent elimination.

Symptoms of bladder stones include straining to urinate, cloudy, smelly urine, blood in the urine, loss of appetite, vomiting, and pain. Early diagnosis is important to prevent permanent kidney damage or even death.

Usually milk, cheese, diary products, and meat must be eliminated from the dog's diet. Vegetables, cereal, and eggs should be substituted. Many vets recommend increasing the dog's water intake even to the point of adding salted broth to its kibble if necessary.

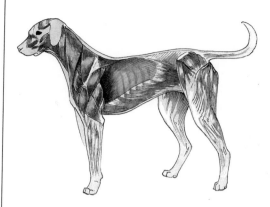

Vigorous daily exercise will help today's dal develop the strong, elegant musculature admired in its ancestors.

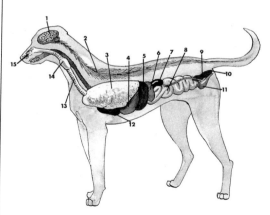

The internal organs of the dalmatian:

| | |
|---|---|
| 1. brain | 9. colon |
| 2. spinal cord | 10. anus |
| 3. lungs | 11. bladder |
| 4. liver | 12. heart |
| 5. stomach | 13. trachea |
| 6. spleen | 14. thyroid cartilage |
| 7. kidney | 15. sinus cavity |
| 8. small intestine | |

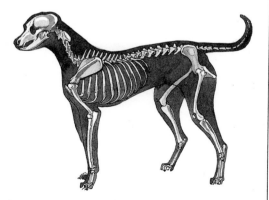

Dalmatian skeleton: Note the well ribbed up chest and long rib cage that provide plenty of breathing room.

# *Understanding Your Dalmatian*

## Life Expectancy of the Dalmatian

At one time people believed that each year in a dog's life was the equivalent of seven years in a human's. In the light of new studies, this scale has been rejected. A new scale of equivalents is now recognized. The greater changes are in the early years.

In the new scale, a six-month-old dog is comparable to a ten-year-old child. A year-old dog is the same age as a fifteen-year-old adolescent. After the first two years, though, each canine year is the equivalent of four human years. Thus a twelve-year-old dog is ready for retirement at age sixty-four. A dog at age twenty-one is an amazing one hundred years old.

| Human-Dog Age Equivalents | |
| --- | --- |
| **Human's Age** | **Dog's Age** |
| 10 years | 6 months |
| 13 years | 8 months |
| 14 years | 10 months |
| 15 years | 1 year |
| 20 years | 18 months |
| 24 years | 2 years |
| 32 years | 4 years |
| 40 years | 6 years |
| 48 years | 8 years |
| 56 years | 10 years |
| 64 years | 12 years |
| 72 years | 14 years |
| 80 years | 16 years |
| 88 years | 18 years |
| 96 years | 20 years |
| 100 years | 21 years |

## Caring for the Elderly Dalmatian

Cancer, heart disease, and kidney disease are three major causes of death in dogs. As the dog ages, hardening of the arteries puts a burden on its heart. In addition, the old dog requires more sleep, is less surefooted, and often loses bladder control.

Older dogs can be kept very comfortable with modern techniques and drugs designed to ease the creaks and groans of age. As owners, we can do our part. Be patient with your old friend. See that your pet has a warm place to sleep in winter and a cool, shaded area in summer. Add a soft pillow to its bed. As you watched over your dal when it was a puppy, don't allow your old pet to overexercise. Try not to make sudden dietary changes. Keep all shots up-to-date. And above all, don't let an older pet run loose near traffic. Hearing goes before sight and smell.

### Saying Goodbye

The question of euthanasia is painful. The pain of an animal who can find no relief from its suffering is pitiable. Many animal lovers believe that an animal living in misery should be allowed a final rest.

Today, several drugs are available for painless euthanasia. When injected into a vein or directly into the heart, the pet is asleep immediately. In a matter of seconds, it is completely unconscious. If you are there, a friend to the end, that end is peaceful and without pain.

## Frequently Asked Questions

### Why Does a Dog Cock Its Leg?

The male dog is marking his territorial boundaries. It makes him feel "at home." Other dogs, passing by, know that a male dog is or has recently been nearby. The spray is nose rather than ground level because it will be more obvious.

### Does Dragging the Rear Mean Worms?

Not necessarily. The problem could be that the dog is trying to express blocked anal glands. If your dog does much of this rump dragging, ask your veterinarian to take a look.

## Why Does My Dog Eat Grass?

When a dog has an upset stomach, long blades of grass irritate the stomach lining and cause vomiting. Acutally, the dog might just enjoy the flavor of new grass.

## How Do You Get Rid of Skunk Scent?

The aroma of a skunk consists of gases that, when exposed to heat, will evaporate. Give your dog a very warm bath with lots of soap, and then a bath in tomato juice or concentrated orange juice. If the scent is on your clothes, don't bury them. Hang them in the hot sun.

## What Is the Best Way To Stop a Dog Fight?

Some dogs are natural neighborhood bullies. This usually is not a problem with dalmatians. First, don't reach for your dog's collar. You may get bitten severely. Try turning a hose on the pair, or a bucket of cold water. As a last resort, try to catch hold of the tail or back leg of either dog and pull. Be careful because the dog may turn on you. Try to throw whichever dog you catch as far as you can. Then get in front of your dog, standing between it and the other. The other dog probably will leave. If the aggressor is yours and the fighting is continuous, castration is one solution that often works.

## Can You Get a Disease from Kissing a Dog?

Probably not. Very few canine germs can be spread by kissing. Nevertheless, kissing should be discouraged. The habit is unsanitary. A kiss transfers what your dog has sniffed or mouthed.

## Do Dogs Dream?

We are not sure. It certainly seems that some dalmatians chase rabbits all night with all the woofing and snorting they do.

## Do Dogs See in Color?

Not as we do. Dogs see in shades of black and white. At most, they might pick up some hues as pastels. A dog can see better than we can at dawn and at dusk. A dalmatian also has a much wider field of vision, almost 270 degrees compared to our 180 degrees.

## Why Do Some Owners Tattoo Their Dogs?

Although many owners provide special pet collars engraved with their own name and telephone number, collars can be lost or removed. One sure way to be certain that your dalmatian can be identified if it strays or is stolen is to have it tattooed. When done by a veterinarian or qualified person, the procedure is quick and generally painless.

Several low-cost national registries offer location services. The American Kennel Club (AKC) offers a free service to its registered owners. When the finder contacts the club, and the dog's AKC registration number was used as identification, for instance, the AKC will contact the owner. If another registry was used, your social security number, for example, the AKC will provide the finder with a list of national registries. Tattooing does not disqualify a dog from participating in AKC-licensed dog shows.

# *Considerations Before You Buy*

## Benefits of Owning a Dog

Ask a dog owner what prompted the decision to get a dog. You'll get a variety of answers. For companionship, many will answer. To teach the children responsibility, some will say. For protection, reply others. Sometimes, "He followed me home, Dad," is enough.

## Your Responsibilities as a Dog Owner

You are embarking on a program of social responsibility when you agree to care for—and to spend money on—a dog. This sensitive, loving animal will be dependent on you for its health, training, and future welfare. As with all major decisions, it's wise to spend a few minutes to recognize the motivation that impelled you toward dog ownership.

Whose idea was it to get a puppy? Was it yours? Why did you decide to get a puppy instead of an adult dog? Were you perhaps looking for a dog as affectionate or as smart as the dog you had when you were growing up?

Whose puppy will it be? Did you get a puppy so your children would learn the responsibility of caring for a pet? Will the children's enthusiasm lag as they get busy with the business of growing up?

Does everyone in the family want a dog? We usually say that the puppy belongs to the one who feeds it. Who will be responsible for training the puppy, cleaning up after it, and making it feel at home? Sometimes a new puppy in the family just means extra work for Mom. Where is this puppy going to eat? In the kitchen? By the back steps? What kind of bowl will it be eating from? What's going to be in that bowl? And when is it coming? If you aren't prompt, you'll hear a low wail, "Isn't it supper time yet?"

Where will the puppy sleep? Inside or outside? At the foot of your bed? In the garage? In a box, on a rug, in a crate? In an outside kennel?

Which veterinarian will you take it to?

It is essential to think about what you expect from your puppy. It is equally important to think about what the puppy itself needs before it arrives. Resolve these questions and others before you bring home that spotted bundle of fur. There are no right or wrong answers.

The right response was the one you made when you decided to read about the breed. Your second response should be to contact other dalmatian owners. Help may be right next door. There is probably an all-breed dog club near you. Attend their next meeting. Ask questions. You will meet new friends. Some may have owned dalmatians for years. You can also write to the secretary of one of the national dog associations for information. Several contact addresses are listed in the back of this book.

## Choosing the Right Dog for You

Some dalmatians are constantly on the move. They like to get up early in the morning and take a fast run around the block. They can maintain that level of activity all day. Some dalmatians prefer a moderate amount of exercise and hate loud noises. Others are strong-minded and inquisitive. They bark at any distraction. Some dals set out on a morning run and then are content to spend the day in whichever room of the house affords the most peace and creature comfort.

Just like their masters, wouldn't you say? The trick is to match the dog's idea of a perfect life to yours.

### Consider Your Life-style

Think about it. If you had to make a choice, would you go for a fast run around the block? Or would you settle down in front of a good movie or ball game on TV?

Will someone be at home all day with the dog or will it spend the day alone?

Do you have children? Are any of the children under age six?

# *Considerations Before You Buy*

Do you have a fenced-in yard? Do you live on a heavily traveled street?

Are there other pets in the family? Dalmatians get along well with cats, horses, and most other dogs.

Again, there are no right or wrong answers. The idea is to decide whether you live a sedentary or an active life-style. Then decide whether that life-style can accommodate a puppy or a grown dog, an active or a quiet new friend.

## Male or Female?

There is a size difference in adult dalmatians. The males, as a rule, are taller and heavier than the females. This, of course, varies among littermates. Your prime considerations should be that the female will have to be given special care twice a year during her estrus (heat) periods. Trainers say a female makes a better watchdog because she is less likely to fight. The adult male, unless neutered, has a greater tendency to roam. It can be distracted by a female in heat.

## Puppy or Grown Dog?

A young puppy is adorable. Watching a puppy develop and actively participating in its training are experiences we will carry with us forever. The knowledge that a young life depends upon us for its very existence can be challenging. That's one reason many people choose to begin with a youngster.

Sometimes, though, a wonderful, loving adult dog is returned to the breeder through no fault of its own. Maybe its family moved into an apartment that didn't allow pets. Perhaps someone developed an allergy. Such "rescued" older dogs are often perfect pets for a family that wants love, affection, and amusement. Often, the ready-made family is the perfect home for an older dog.

An adult dalmatian can be less work for everyone. An adult normally doesn't require housebreaking. It usually is past the chewing stage, and trained not to bark or get on furniture.

## Pet or Show Quality?

If you look forward to a show career for your dalmatian, buy the best dog you can afford from a breeder you like and trust.

Purebred puppies are graded against a standard of perfection. Some breeders can spot a potential show dog right away. Most check the puppy over a period of several months before making a firm statement. A dog with show potential will cost more initially, including perhaps an overnight stay in another city.

Most of us are going to be very happy with a "pet" dog. Pet-quality dogs are given the same care, vaccinations, and deworming as the rest of the litter.

Some dalmatians go through the "puppy-uglies" when at certain growth periods the head and legs seem to be out of proportion. From six to eight weeks of age is a good time to choose a dalmatian puppy. A puppy that is well balanced at this age usually will return to that balance later.

## Purchasing a Dalmatian

There are many sources for purebred dogs. Kennels advertise in national magazines. Pet stores display appealing puppies. Home breeders post signs in veterinarians' offices and in "pet market" newspaper columns. What is a conscientious potential owner to do?

First, ask your veterinarian for advice. Ask about any local breeders. These dedicated fans of the breed are often scrupulously attentive to their dogs. Contact a local dog fanciers group. Attend a dog show. Talk to your neighbors. Visit as many kennels and pet shops as you can. Are the premises clean? Are there any dogs with runny noses? Diarrhea? Do the owners seem knowledgeable?

## How Much Will a Dalmatian Cost?

Owning a dog is not inexpensive. The new owner should be prepared to provide food, water, and health care in addition to affection and comfort. Of these five obligations, food and health care are the most costly.

A show-quality dalmatian will cost almost twice as much as one judged pet quality. If you are willing to make the drive, those purchased from country kennels are usually less costly than their big city cousins.

Your veterinarian can help you. Not only will a veterinarian suggest ways to reduce your initial outlay, many will offer advice on diet, vitamins, and training. You will be instructed on procedures you can do at home, such as deworming, to reduce the need for successive office visits.

## Veterinarian Approval

You should take your new puppy to a veterinarian within 24 hours of purchase for a well-puppy checkup. When you need veterinary services later, your vet will have a baseline upon which to make decisions.

Most dedicated breeders will stand behind their puppy up to two weeks after purchase. This could include assuming some portion of medical expenses. It also could include replacing a sick puppy with a healthy one. If you are not offered this choice, you should ask. If you are refused, you have a right to take your business elsewhere.

A thoughtful breeder also will give you written guarantees against hereditary diseases.

### How To Choose a Veterinarian

Talk to your neighbors. Try to select a veterinarian near your neighborhood. In an emergency, travel time is very important. Check with your local breed club, if one is available. Ask members of the local kennel club for recommendations. You are looking for someone in whom you can place your trust and confidence.

Then, walk up to the office door and go in. Talk to the staff. Are they professional looking and acting? Are they friendly? Ask to look at the kennels. Are they clean? Ask about fees. Are they reasonable?

Once you have selected your veterinarian, a special relationship is born. James Herriot made millions of friends with his gentle "Wise and Wonderful" series. Your veterinarian can be your and your dog's best friend.

## When Can I Bring My Puppy Home?

The standard answer, of course, is you can bring your puppy home when it can eat and thrive physically and emotionally away from its mother and littermates. For most puppies, that works out to between seven and nine weeks of age.

If you have children under age six, you might want to select an already socialized puppy nine to twelve weeks old. Because behaviorists have proven that it is important for the puppy to make human friends early, your breeder will see to it that the puppy receives the attention it requires.

## The "Forty-nine Day" Theory

Are you beginning to read articles about breeders who say, "I positively will not allow any puppy to leave its mother until it is forty-nine days old."? What is this forty-ninth day business?

Dog behaviorists have demonstrated that a puppy must live in a litter long enough to "learn how to be a dog." In the early weeks of life, the puppy does not stray far from its mother and littermates. Sometime between the ages of five and seven weeks, though, the puppy will recognize a human voice and respond to it. It is around the seven-week-old mark (forty-nine days) that a human, preferably the new owner, can and should take over. Studies show that the puppy forms a strong and lasting relationship with the person who feeds, comforts, plays with, and trains it during the critical socialization age of seven to twelve weeks.

# *Your Dalmatian Puppy*

## Before You Bring Your Puppy Home

Congratulations! You have made an important and long-lasting decision. The right puppy will be a joy to own. From the beginning, your puppy will try to be a participant in whatever you do. It will adapt to your life-style. It will submerge its identity in yours. If you watch television, your puppy will want to settle down on the rug beside you. If you get in the car, your new friend will want to jump in too. You're both lucky, you have taken the first steps on the journey to a long and enviable relationship. Now, what plans do you have for your life together?

Imagine that you are bringing home a new baby. Now imagine yourself standing in the middle of the living room with the baby in your arms. Would you wonder: Where on earth will we put this baby? Does anybody here know anything about taking care of babies? What will the baby eat tonight? Where will it sleep? Of course not. You and your family will have been ready for a long time. And so it should be with your new puppy. Be ready when it arrives.

There is just one special difference in this new friend of yours. The puppy is not really a member of the human family. In some cases, you can and should treat a puppy differently from the other family members. It has different food needs, and special training and exercise requirements. What is more important, your dalmatian will thrive on this difference.

## Supply Checklist

There is no need to purchase all of the cute items in the pet store. Not at one time, anyway. Do you remember the story of the little boy who was given every toy he wanted for his birthday? An hour after the party, his parents peeked in. Which toy do you think the little boy was playing with? That's right, he was playing with the boxes the toys were packed in.

Your puppy's needs are simple. The following basic items will help it to feel loved. When the puppy arrives at your home it would appreciate:
- its own food dish,
- its own water bowl,
- its own bed, and
- a chew toy.

I am sure that later you will want to expand this list to include collars and leads, toys, grooming utensils, shampoos, and brushes, for instance. But for now, this short list will do. The most important on the list is you. A puppy needs love and affection and a few basics to call its own.

## A Place To Sleep and a Place To Eat

Like many of us, a dog is a creature of habit. Puppies, in particular, appreciate consistency.

Set a regular feeding schedule and stick to it. Supper hour shouldn't be flexible. I know you wouldn't feed your puppy supper at 5:30 Monday afternoon, for instance, and then make it wait until 9:00 Tuesday night for another meal. Neither should you feed it in the kitchen one morning and on the back porch the next. When selecting a feeding station, try to find one spot that will be convenient for you. Water should be readily available.

The puppy should have a water bowl and an eating dish all its own. Both can be as inexpensive as metal pans from the feed store. Many owners purchase heavy stoneware crocks. Others prefer a set of stainless steel bowls set in stands to keep them off the floor. The important guidelines are: The dishes should be heavy enough so the puppy can't drag them around and sturdy enough so the puppy can't chew them up.

Many breeders send their puppies off to new homes with a three-day supply of food. It is best for the puppy's digestion that diet changes be made gradually. If you do intend to change the puppy's diet, introduce the new food over a period of four days. The first day, feed three-fourths of the puppy's old diet, for instance, and one-fourth new food. The next day, make the proportions half-and-half. By day three, the puppy is eating three-fourths new food and one-fourth original diet. Day four, you're through. Feed the new diet exclusively.

## The Big Day

The big day is finally here! It is time to bring your puppy home. If possible, bring someone with you. On the trip home, one could drive and the other could hold and comfort the puppy.

If the dam is on the premises, bring a *mama towel* with you when you go to pick up the puppy. A mama towel is going to be the puppy's first touch of home. Find a large, soft towel. Do you have a tattered beach towel? That's just the right size. You'll use this towel as a throw mat on your rug, for after-bath rubdowns, and for comforting.

Give the towel to the owners of the puppy's mother. Ask them to rub the mother's face and head with the towel. You want the towel to pick up just enough of Mama's scent to make the puppy feel at home.

When you return to the car, spread the mama towel on your lap or on the car seat beside you. Put the puppy on the towel and speak to it softly. If you're lucky, the puppy will sleep most of the way home.

Most kennel owners don't feed a puppy just before its first trip. This is probably a good idea. A carsick puppy takes a long time to get over its distrust of cars. Consequently, if you and your puppy arrive home in the middle of the afternoon, it will be tired, confused, and hungry.

First, though, your puppy probably will want to relieve itself. Put the puppy down in the yard near the special spot you chose ahead of time. Speak to it in a low, friendly voice. If the puppy does use that spot, be generous with your praise.

Then, if your dalmatian will be a house dog, open the door and welcome your puppy home. Let the puppy wander around a bit. Get the puppy used

to the sounds and smells of its new family. Not too many sounds, though. Is the noise level too high? It would be better if the puppy could have some time to get used to its new surroundings without being held too much. Put the mama towel in its crate. Try to get the puppy to lie down. Sit beside it. Quietly stroke its back. Touch the puppy with a light, feathery motion. Tickle-touch the front of its chest. Play with its ears, its paws. If your puppy settles down to sleep, it has taken the first step toward accepting you as its best friend. From now on, you literally won't take a step alone.

## Staying Alone

In direct relationship to the bonding that takes place during the day, the first few nights will be hard for both of you. Unless you plan to let the puppy sleep in your room instead of its own, you have to teach it to spend the night alone, quietly.

Now, if you like the idea of a dog sleeping in your room, or in your bed, by all means, allow it. Do remember, though, that one day your little puppy will weigh 50 or 60 pounds (23–27 kg). And at that point, if you change your mind about where it is to sleep, you will have a struggle ahead of you.

If you want your puppy to have its own space as you have yours, now is the time to start training. Your puppy will moan, wail, bark, yelp, scratch on the door, be inconsiderate, and ignore your threats. For two, maybe three nights, you must be hard-hearted. Close your ears. Think of the puppy as a baby. If a baby's parents didn't insist that the baby stay in its own bed, they could wind up having a third bed partner for years.

The first few days that your dal is adapting to its new family, try to remember that it also misses its kennel family. For seven or eight weeks your puppy lived and ate and slept and played and fought with a noisy, competitive litter. Naturally, it will miss the action. Surely, it is bewildered. Absolutely, it doesn't like being alone. After all, its mother and brothers and sisters always piled into bed too.

Without a doubt, your puppy will cry and tell you that it is lonesome. And it is.

## The First Night

Dalmatian puppies are equipped with the saddest, most lonesome wail you've ever heard. This musical, keening lamentation announces the puppy's misery to the whole house. It is hard to ignore. Do your best not to go in the first time or two the puppy calls. Give it a chance to settle down.

If the puppy insists that you return, go in, speak to it quietly and stroke it. Stay until the puppy is calm, and leave again. Be very matter-of-fact about leaving. Close the door. Go far enough away that the puppy is sure you're gone. You needn't go too far, though. It probably will start to complain again in a few minutes. Return to the room. Talk to the puppy. Be sure to stay until the puppy is calm. Then leave again. The puppy must get the idea that this is where it stays.

If, after two or three attempts, soothing words don't work, wait outside the closed door and when the puppy starts to fuss, knock sharply on the door. Or clap your hands and call out, "No!"

The theory is that you don't want to give the puppy the idea that if it makes enough noise you will return to free it from this terrible lonesomeness. Instead, make sure the puppy associates its fussing with your displeasure. In the morning, praise the puppy heartily for being such a good puppy all night.

The seven-week-old puppy has some control over its bladder. If it fusses a lot, be sure it doesn't have to eliminate. Usually, if you take the puppy outside about 10 P.M., and pick up its water dish, it will be comfortable until early the next morning— very early the next morning.

### Music to Its Ears

One puppy owner leaves a radio on in the puppy's room overnight. The soft sound soothes her lonesome little friend. Another swears by an old ticking clock wrapped in the mama towel. One inventive owner wrapped a hot water bottle in one of her old T-shirts and placed it in the puppy's bed. She says she never heard a peep out of the puppy all night! I wish it had been that easy for some of our puppies. Mostly, our family just had to grin and bear it (and shut our ears to the complaints) for a few nights.

### First Lessons

By the time you bring your puppy home it probably will be seven or eight weeks old. Within days, the two of you already will be well on your way to that special friendship. If yours is an inside puppy, you have had your share of accidents and misadventures. Never mind. You expected them.

Now is the time to get in some quality training time. First of all, teach the puppy its name. Use pleasant associations. Don't call "Puppy, puppy, puppy," like the breeder did in the kennel. Everybody came to that one. Use your puppy's name often. Say "Dotty, come!" and "What a good girl Dotty is!"

Richard Wolters, one of today's top trainers, tells us that at about eight or nine weeks the puppy itself will tell you the exact day it is ready for that first lesson. That will be the day the puppy responds to its name.

To test the puppy, choose a time it is lying quietly, but paying no attention to you. Without a lot of fanfare, call the puppy by name. If the puppy keeps on chewing or scratching or whatever, let it be. Try again the next day. The first time the puppy stops what it is doing and looks up at you as if to say, "Yes?" you're both ready for a new adventure. As Wolters says, "When this happens, at that moment (the puppy is) ready to accept his first training . . . and the results will be spectacular."

Use these early months of puppyhood to teach relationships, loyalty, house manners, and doggie etiquette. Serious obedience training, usually thought of as "sit," "come," "heel," "stay," and "down," can't be started until the puppy has some control over itself, usually around seven months. These commands are covered in the chapter, Training Your Dalmatian (see page 43).

The puppy will learn soon enough that a loud "no" or pointed finger or a loud hand clap means "stop it." Stop barking, stop getting on the sofa, stop chewing up the newspaper, just *stop* doing whatever it is you're doing.

Next, the puppy should learn that you're the boss. You're the leader of the pack. Enforce this lesson by being very sure the puppy obeys you. If you don't want the puppy on the sofa, for instance, say "no" or "off" (anything but "down"; save "down" for "lie down"). Be firm. The puppy must understand that it either jumps off the sofa immediately or you will lift it off. Either way, your order must be obeyed.

Don't forget the final training rule. Even if you have to lift or push or help the puppy off the sofa, once it is on the floor, praise it. Praise it imme-

To avoid confrontations, be sure that your dal has a place to call its own. The command is: "No Dotty. Off, now!"

diately and thoroughly. Use your most loving, friendly voice. From the puppy's point of view it deserves the praise. After all, it's on the floor, and it's not misbehaving anymore, is it?

## How Puppies Learn

The first rule in training puppies is there are no hard and fast rules. All puppies cannot be handled in the same way. Each puppy is an individual. Your puppy's character, its disposition, its abilities, affect how it will learn. Some guidelines, though, will apply to all puppies.

In the first place, a dog has a great instinctual need to master or to be mastered. Your dalmatian will look for a pack leader in its new home. Once the two of you agree that you will be the "leader of the pack," a certain orderliness takes place in your relationship.

Second, remember that a dalmatian is sensitive. Harsh methods won't work. You will find that the more positive your training, and the less often you have to correct your puppy, the quicker it will learn. Discipline your puppy fairly, praise it exuberantly, train it with kindness.

Third, remember that your puppy cannot understand words as words. Because of this, it pays attention to your tone of voice, your body language, and your moods. Think of this as cause and effect.

Within its ability to reason, a puppy thinks, "You say 'sit' (cause), I sit (effect), and you are pleased. I love to please you."

Often your puppy doesn't understand what you want. It may not be paying attention. It may try to lick your face instead. Work harder. It wants to please you.

Everybody is happy when the puppy pays attention: "You say 'sit,' this time I sit, you are pleased and you praise me and hug me. Nothing to it. I sit because I love to be praised," the puppy learns.

This cause and effect learning leads us to the final rule. Let's say you come home one afternoon and find that your puppy has been at war with a sofa pillow.

22

# Your Dalmatian Puppy

Because your dog associates one event with the action that precedes it, don't discipline the puppy for chewing on the pillow. You can take the puppy to the pillow if you want to. You can hold the pillow up to its nose and fuss and make a lot of noise. The puppy will slink away from you and look miserable. But don't think you have taught it not to chew the pillow. What your puppy learned was that sometimes when you come home you are a grouch. For this reason, trainers tell us to go to the puppy to discipline it. Never call it to you. Remember the get off the sofa lesson? Your puppy obeyed the most recent command, didn't it? It came. So why would you fuss?

## No Jumping

Nobody likes a dog that jumps up. Ladderlike stockings, muddy footprints, and embedded white hairs on a clean trouser leg can ruin the most amiable disposition.

The best way to stop a puppy from jumping is to start early. "No jumping" is taught outside, on the grass. When your puppy starts to jump up, open your hand and spread your fingers in front of its nose. Say firmly, "no jumping!" Walk on. Because this isn't a one-time-and-you-learn-it procedure, be ready. Repeat the procedure three or four times. The puppy may learn quickly.

If your puppy hasn't learned, go to phase two. The next time the puppy starts to jump, spread your fingers, say "no jumping," and lift your knee to the puppy's chest. The puppy will tumble backwards. It probably will pick itself up and look up at you as if to wonder what happened. Lean over and soothe the puppy. Pet it and talk to it. Act as if you have no idea why it fell over. Keep on walking. It won't be long before the puppy will jump and paw at the air around you, not on you. A dalmatian puppy is much too bright to turn unexpected somersaults.

## Look, I'm Sitting

Long before you would think so, your puppy can anticipate what you want it to do. Perhaps it's a puppy game. Even so, turn the game to your advantage.

A three-month-old dalmatian can learn to sit when looking forward to a treat. Start with the puppy's food bowl. Pick up the bowl. Fill it. The puppy knows that mealtime is at hand. It will be watching your every move. Hold the bowl above the puppy's head. Say, "sit." The puppy's instinct will be to jump. Don't give in. The puppy will probably sit, trying to figure out what to do next. Catch this indecision. The instant the puppy looks like it's going to sit, say "sit," praise heartily, and put the bowl down. You will be amazed at how quickly your dal will learn to sit for supper.

Once the puppy has a little practice, you will have no trouble getting a "sit" anytime.

## How To Treat Your Puppy

An eight-week-old dalmatian will weigh between 13 and 20 pounds (6–9 kg). Many adults have trouble controlling a squirming, wiggling 20-pound puppy. Children, in particular, cannot cope. Trying to love the puppy, they find a convenient handle, usually the front legs, and pull the puppy up to their level. The puppy squirms and escapes. Sometimes the puppy is lucky and lands on its feet. Sometimes it lands on its head. The puppy squeals and runs away. Your child runs after it. What do you do now?

## Lifting and Carrying

Children under age six can be taught to sit beside the puppy instead of raising the puppy up to their eye level. From this position, they can pat the puppy on the head and rub its ears. They can roll a ball for the puppy. Teach younger children that little puppies love to be fingerstroked. Teach them to scratch lightly under the puppy's chin, down its chest, behind its ears, and along the top of its tail.

Why don't you try sitting on the floor too? Your dalmatian is a curious, intelligent animal. It will romp right over to you, inspect your shoelaces and untie them faster than you can say, "Look here."

# Your Dalmatian Puppy

Use both hands when lifting your dalmatian puppy. Place one hand against the rib cage and the other beneath the rear legs.

Then it will scamper off again only to return a few seconds later.

Older children and adults, too, should be taught how to pick up a puppy. A reminder from you will make your puppy's life easier and avoid permanent injury. A puppy should be held with one hand firmly under the chest and a second hand supporting its heavy little rump. Never let anyone pick up the puppy by the scruff of the neck or with one hand under the abdomen.

## Tone of Voice

A dog cannot understand much of what you say. It can always, however, understand the tone in which you say it. Trainers often single out two important rules for talking to dogs. One is consistency in the words you use. The second is a definite change in your tone of voice. Always use the same word or words with a firm, authoritative tone of voice when correcting. If you want your puppy to stop doing something, don't confuse the puppy by

saying "Stop that!" "Puppy, quit it!" "No, Spot!" or "No!" A simple "no" is better.

Second, be sure your praise voice is markedly different from your disciplinary voice. Cultivate a happy, singing tone to praise the puppy. Raise your pitch, put a lilt in your voice. Make that puppy know that you think it is the brightest, best doggie in the world. "What a good dog!" chanted by a loving voice is music to a puppy's ears.

## Punishing

When your puppy deserves it, you should punish it fairly and promptly. The puppy must learn that when it has done something wrong you are displeased. Because we are working under the assumption that your puppy wants very much to please you, let's examine the world from the puppy's point of view.

A dog has a very limited memory. Suppose it makes an error, refusing to come when called, for instance. *When* you react to the error is as important as *how* you react. If the puppy runs off when you want it to come, it very likely will return to you wagging its tail. It is ready to share with you its wonderful experiences on the road. Now is not the time to punish your puppy for running off. It surely will not understand why. From the puppy's point of view, it has returned to its most favorite person in the world. What happens? This favorite person yells at it.

Remember, no matter how annoyed you might be, greet your puppy happily and love it for returning. Then, work—on a leash—with the command "come" as soon as possible.

## Socialization

The dalmatian is a social animal by nature. It will bond to you. It will want to be with you at all times. Your puppy will jump up when you open the door, cry if it can't follow you. Within the limits of its understanding it will obey you. This dependence is part of a puppy's charm.

At some point, though, you will want to extend

this obedience to other people. Particularly, you will want your puppy to stand still for its doctor. How will the veterinarian be able to look in its ears, listen to its heart, or examine its stomach if your puppy jumps and barks and snaps at fingers? You certainly want your puppy to behave if you enter it in a puppy show and the judge steps in for a closer look. How will the judge recognize its beautiful conformation?

Begin the puppy's introductory social skills by playing with it. Remember the "get down on the floor" suggestions? Roll your puppy over on its back and tickle-stroke its tummy. Put the puppy on your lap. Touch its little paws. Separate the soft footpads. Stroke its smooth ear leather with your fingers. Hold its little face and look into its eyes. Make the puppy feel good that you are holding it. It probably will get very quiet, blissfully enjoying the attention from the one person it wants to please more than anyone else in the world. When the veterinarian or the technician or the judge makes a similar examination, your puppy will be easier to handle.

## The Right Toys

It is important to offer the right toy. Don't give the puppy lightweight plastic to chew on. A dalmatian will demolish such toys within an hour, swallow, and possibly choke on the pieces. Avoid those "squeak" toys with whistles or noisemakers that might break off and be swallowed, too. If a toy seems too cute to pass up, allow the puppy to play with some of the sturdier ones under close supervision by you. At the very least, remove the whistle and inspect the toy frequently. When the toy shows signs of wear, replace it.

My puppies loved an old cotton sock, knotted around a canning jar ring. The ring made a satisfactory noise and an easy carry handle. I would avoid giving the puppy an old shoe. No telling what will happen if the puppy can't tell the difference between its old slipper and your new tennis shoes. It's best not to put temptation in the puppy's way.

Usually, veterinarians recommend bones made of hard plastics. You should be cautious, though, of giving extremely hard bones to puppies. Some of these products are so hard that puppies' teeth have been chipped.

## Teething and Chewing

A puppy will chew. Nobody raises puppies without a story or two to tell. Every little plant leaf that waves, every dainty chair leg that beckons, every ball that rolls must be chased and subdued. This is fine for the ball, but is hard on the other two.

The young puppy must be kept away from dangerous houseplants, such as philodendron, Boston ivy, and azaleas. Dangling electrical wires, coffee-table books, and throw pillows are tempting targets.

Sometimes it's easier to move temptation out of the way for awhile. When our children were toddlers, my husband and I child proofed the family room. We cleared the breakables from coffee tables and low book shelves. We added support to wobbly table legs and did away with dangling venetian blind cords.

We carried out this "it's easier to pick it up, don't run yourself ragged" theory with puppies. Certainly children and puppies should learn better. But I think that while you are training, it's easier if you pick up items that hang down, wave, rustle, or

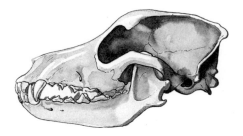

The dalmatian's sharp scissors bite will make short work of wooden stair steps, leather tie-out leashes, and waving blossoms.

otherwise attract attention to themselves. Then, after two months or so (with puppies, anyway) you should be able to replace your treasures one at a time.

## Housetraining Your Puppy

Some dalmatians live outside from the beginning. For these owners, housebreaking is a breeze. A dal loves the outdoors. It is accustomed to eliminating outside. The outdoor dal likes the feel of grass and leaves under its feet. It seems uncomfortable walking on slippery floors. It will not want to come in unless the temperature is freezing cold or smothering hot, or unless it is lonesome. It comes inside because that is where its owner is. If its owner goes out, the dal will follow immediately.

Nevertheless, because we enjoy their company as much as they seem to enjoy ours, a great many dalmatians do seem to wind up as house dogs. Here is where the problem begins. Housebreaking an indoor puppy of any breed can be a time-consuming and frustrating chore. The puppy must be trained to newspaper, or it must be coaxed to wait until it is outside.

## Paper Training

First, select a special spot, inside or outside the house, where the puppy should eliminate.

Second, don't let your puppy wander through the house unsupervised. Keep it next to you every minute of the day. If you're really busy, attach one end of a lead to the puppy and the other to your belt or your wrist. It's far better to have a week or two of restriction than a lifetime of corrections.

Third, be alert. Be especially aware during the critical moments shortly after meals and when the puppy wakes up. A puppy normally will urinate after every meal, every nap, and every play session. Carry the puppy to its paper or outside.

Fourth, watch for signs of interest during the in-between times: Is your puppy sniffing along the floor, walking in circles? A puppy will sniff around

Be patient. Stay alert. The puppy will get the idea very soon. Praise any success.

first, wanting to do its business in a familiar "spot." It is much better for all concerned to have its spot one that you have selected already. When the puppy relieves itself in the right place, praise and sing and be happy.

Convincing your little friend to use your chosen spot instead of one it prefers can take some doing.

Top: A dalmatian is very comfortable living out-of-doors, but provide it with an enclosed run if the entire yard is not fenced. A long lead is not a good solution. Bottom: Your dal will be happier if you always feed it at the same time and in the same place.

# *Your Dalmatian Puppy*

Try sponging up a little of its urine with a sheet of newspaper. Spread this "scented" paper on top of three or four clean, double-page sheets of paper. Bring the puppy to the paper each time you think it should be ready to relieve itself.

Then, remove the top, wettest paper and dispose of it. Put fresh newspaper on the bottom. Place one slightly damp sheet on top. Every time you clean up, leave one paper with its own damp scent on top of the pile. Soon the puppy will head for the scented paper of its own accord. Its aim might be off, but it will have taken a step in the right direction. Within a week, barring accidents, your puppy will be "double-page paper-trained." You still can expect to find accidents until the puppy matures completely.

Sometime between three and four months of age, you will want to transfer your paper-trained puppy to the outside. This should not be a big problem. The puppy is a lot older.

Pick up a sheet of the puppy's wet paper. Take the sheet outside and place it at the location you chose. Lead the puppy to the spot. It should eliminate on the paper. This transferal is learned easily. Within a day or two, you shouldn't have to bring the paper outside anymore.

## Crate Training

There are two ways to crate train. Both are for "house puppies." Both, in my opinion, are better and easier and surer than old-fashioned paper training.

The first technique is designed for use by those owners who will be at home with the puppy for most of the first two weeks. The second is for those who must train a puppy that will be left alone all day.

◀ "Fetch" is a game that must be taught. Eventually, your dal will figure out that if it doesn't return the ball to you, it doesn't get to play anymore.

A crate is a wonderful place for a rambunctious puppy to spend a few hours. An older dog will appreciate the peace and quiet.

**Basic Crate Training:** Crate training, although the most efficient method of housebreaking, is initially more time-consuming for the owner. The point of the training is that once in its crate, the puppy will do its best not to soil its den. It will wait for you to come. Even a six- or seven-week-old puppy will bark and whine for you to let it out if you don't get back soon enough.

Try to select a location along a wall or in a corner where the puppy can see and hear the activity of the house, but is out of the mainstream of traffic. The crate should contain nothing but a washable mat for the puppy to lie down on, and perhaps a chew toy. No food or water.

Put the puppy in the crate. Go about your business. Talk to it while you work, but don't hover over the crate. Leave the puppy in the crate no longer than ten minutes. Then pick it up and play with it, cuddle it, feed it, or whatever you wish, and then put it back in the crate for another ten minutes or so. It may go to sleep. After all, little puppies sleep lots more than they are awake.

If the puppy is sleeping, let it sleep until it wakes up. When it wakes up, go to it immediately. Pick up the puppy and take it to its paper. Then, spend some time with the puppy. Depending on the time of day, play with it or feed it or take it outside.

Crate time is lengthened gradually. At about sixteen weeks of age, the puppy's maximum daytime stay is extended to about two hours. This depends on your puppy and its own schedule. You can learn by watching the puppy for signs of discomfort.

## If You Are Away from Home All Day

These days, when both caregivers often work away from home, housebreaking a puppy can be difficult. Some actions can be taken, however, to make even this experience easier all around. If your situation is such that you must leave the puppy alone in the house, by all means, crate train.

Select a small room with an easily cleaned floor. A laundry room, bathroom, or kitchen would be ideal. The theory is to divide the puppy's small world into three parts. Place the crate in one corner of the room. Spread newspaper in an opposite corner. As in paper training, leave a scented page on top. In a third corner place the puppy's water bowl and food dish. Put the puppy in the crate, but leave the crate door open. At least it will learn to appreciate the crate's security. It will leave the crate to eliminate.

Although crate training is the easiest, fastest way to housebreak a puppy, some people object to crating. They picture their puppy in a "cage" because they project their own human feelings onto a pet. Such well-meaning owners usually think of zoos and circuses where cages are used primarily for animal restraint.

**Understanding the Denning Instinct:** Let's look at the crate from the dog's point of view for a minute. Your dalmatian, though it doesn't resemble its wolf ancestors as much as some of its canine cousins do, is a den animal. Today's crate provides indoor dogs with the security of a den. Because its primitive instincts are strong, they control many of the dog's modern habits. As it has for centuries, it will share the companionship of a hearth and fire

with its human friends. It will walk in circles before lying down to sleep. It will lie down facing the entrance.

Many of my doggy friends gladly retreat to their crates when the household noise level is too high. Some have even been known to pull the door shut behind them. "Go away, world," they seem to say; "I need my peace and quiet."

**Hints on Selecting a Crate:** Crates, usually made either of metal or fiberglass, are available at pet supply stores and from catalogs. Do you plan to travel with your dal? Some crates are collapsible and, thus, portable.

Unless you want to buy another in four months, the crate should be large enough for a grown dalmation to stand up in. This means that for comfort, most dalmatians need a crate about 3 feet (.9 m) square and at least 30 inches (73 cm) high. This gives the dog room to turn around, change its position, stretch out.

## Accidents

Your puppy will have an occasional accident until it is six months old. If the puppy leaves a puddle or a pile in the house where it is not supposed to, work harder at understanding why. Did you not get back in time? Is there a disruption in its life? Do you have a new baby or another dog? Go back to basics. Watch the puppy more carefully. Rubbing the puppy's nose in its mess is disgusting, confusing, and unfair. And hitting the puppy won't help because it won't understand. Just try harder to catch it in the act.

The minute the objectionable behavior begins, try what we call the "swoop" technique of training. Reach the puppy as quickly as possible. Even while you're on the way, call out "no!" in a loud voice. "Swoop" the puppy up even though it's still dribbling and carry it to the paper or outside, repeating, "no!" Once or at most twice should teach the lesson.

**After the Accident:** Even the best-mannered puppy, and older dog, too, will have an occasional indoor accident. Later, you may be sure the puppy will search out that very spot for a repeat performance.

Generations of puppy owners have shared a few tips you may find helpful. The most obvious is to keep the puppy on washable vinyl or wooden floors. Second, they suggest you install a gate to be sure the puppy doesn't stray. The third tip is to clean up any mistakes right away.

If the puppy does wander onto your wall-to-wall carpet, an old fashioned solution for urine stains is plain old cornstarch. First, blot the spot with paper towels. Use your foot and press hard. Change paper towels several times until you are sure the moisture is gone. Then layer a generous amount of cornstarch over the spot. Leave the cornstarch on overnight. Keep the puppy away from it. Once the cornstarch is dry, just vacuum it up. The only caution here is to be very sure the spot is very dry. If not, you'll make paste. Otherwise, it works like a charm.

Several companies manufacture an enzymatic stain and odor remover. Used immediately on carpets and upholstered furniture, an enzyme will eliminate the problem of "repeats."

Here's another remedy. This time be sure the rug is colorfast; test a small corner. First, blot up all the liquid you can. Then, mix one part of vinegar with two parts of water. Saturate the spot with the mixture. Blot the spot with a pad of paper towels. Then mix 1 teaspoon (5 ml) dishwashing detergent with 1 cup (250 ml) warm water. Cover with a pad of paper towels and weigh down. Let dry.

Don't use a product with ammonia to clean a urine stain. It's the ammonia odor that you're trying to get rid of.

**Disposing of Waste:** If you walk your puppy on a leash, remember to be fair to other strollers. Curb your dog. Never let your puppy eliminate on the sidewalk. And pick up after your puppy. Many owners carry a clean-up scoop. Others, in a gesture to modern convenience, tuck a small plastic storage baggie in a jacket pocket. At cleanup time, place the baggie over one hand, inside out. Reach down, collect the waste, reverse the bag and snap it closed. Deposit the bag in a refuse container.

# Living with Your Dalmatian

## Day by Day with Your Dalmatian

A healthy dalmatian puppy will eat well. It will look nice and lean and will be well muscled. Its eyes will be clear and free of irritation. Its ears will perk up when you talk to it. The inquiring tilt of its head signals intelligence and interest. Its short, hard coat will be sleek and glossy, the background color a soft pure white. It will be frisky and friendly to family and alert with strangers.

## Grooming Needs

The dalmatian needs no stripping or plucking or docking as is necessary in other breeds. Unless your dalmatian has investigated something particularly odoriferous, bathing is not necessary more than three or four times a year.

Some dals are extremely susceptible to skin irritations. It is important that you do what you can to keep your dalmatian's coat in top condition. This may mean paying closer attention to little problems before they develop into major worries.

It is important to keep a dalmatian brushed. The stiff white hairs are being replaced continually, giving the dalmatian's coat its sleek, shiny look. Because old, dead hair is irritating, you should remove it frequently. Using a moderate bristle brush, brush with the lay of the coat. Given a daily or every other day brushing with a moderately firm bristle brush, the dalmatian will be basically odor free.

If your dalmatian sheds excessively, scratches, or has bald spots, rule out mange and allergies. Then consider its diet. Add one to two teaspoons of fat to its daily meal. Try gently rubbing your dalmatian's skin with vitamin E oil or wheat germ oil. Some breeders have success with lanolin cream. Be observant. Dogs have allergies just as people do.

If your dalmatian is a house dog, take a look at those toenail tips once a week or so, and keep them well trimmed. If you can hear a click when the dog walks on a wooden floor, it's time for a trim.

**Bathing:** A healthy dalmatian should be bathed very infrequently, at most three or four times a year. The dalmatian's skin contains oil glands that protect the coat and help keep it water resistant. Overbathing removes natural oils.

Many dog groomers report that flea-control shampoos tend to yellow the hair on light-haired dogs. Most "people" shampoos are too acidic. Therefore, when you do bathe your dalmatian, use a good commercial dog shampoo.

First, a dog doesn't need or appreciate water in its ears or eyes. Crumple a small wad of cotton and lightly plug each ear. Place a dab of eye ointment in each eye. You can buy it in a pet store or at your veterinarian's office.

Lather and rinse the head first. Wet the dog thoroughly. Work your way down the dog's back, legs, feet, and tail.

The secret to a clean wash is a thorough rinse. Rinse and rinse some more. Sometimes special rinses are used to "bring out the white" in show dogs. I wouldn't recommend using on your dalmatian any rinse that contains vinegar, lemon, or bleach.

Unless the day is exceptionally warm and sunny, dry the dog carefully and completely before letting it go outside. The dalmatian's short coat dries quickly. Nevertheless, if the weather is really cold, try shampooing in the evening. That way the dog's coat has overnight to dry.

## Collar and Lead

At some point after the puppy has settled in, you should introduce it to a collar. When you're at the veterinarian's office for one of the puppy-shot visits, ask for a 1-inch (2.5 cm) wide webbed collar. These come in attractive colors. The primary colors are good-looking and comfortable for a dalmatian. Any color collar is indispensable for training. While you're at it, pick out a 6-foot (1.8 m) long, lightweight webbed leash, also.

When you get home, put the collar on the puppy for a couple of hours. It probably won't like the

# *Living with Your Dalmatian*

unaccustomed weight, but this is one of the many times you should hold firm. A collar is necessary. Take it off after a few hours if your puppy really objects, but try again the next day. After awhile, the puppy won't even notice the collar.

Then you can attach the lead. Let your puppy walk around the house with the leash on. Watch to see that the leash doesn't get tangled and choke the puppy. The puppy may play with the leash and chew on it. It may scratch at it and act annoyed for awhile. Eventually the puppy will ignore both the collar and lead. You, of course, have to be alert and available at all times in case the lead gets tangled in something.

Remember to check the fit of the collar often while your puppy is still growing. You should be able to slip at least two fingers underneath a properly sized collar.

## Indoor Space Requirements

Many dalmatians live indoors with the family. Most dog owners would agree that both the family and the puppy are happier if the newcomer follows house rules. These rules are easier to enforce if the puppy has its own space.

Although you will make the final decision, let's see what space your puppy would choose. In the first place, the puppy instinctively would seek a dry, sheltered location, preferably against a wall, in a corner, or under a table. It would want to be out of a draft. And it would want to be wherever you are.

Every year many puppies are injured seriously because they are underfoot. In its effort to stay as close to you as possible, a new puppy might pick a spot right in front of the refrigerator. When the family moves into the living room at night, the puppy will follow to lie at your feet. It's up to you to guide the puppy to its own bed.

What kind of bed are we talking about? Wicker baskets are enchanting, and puppies look adorable in them. I wouldn't recommend a basket for your dalmatian, because the puppy will shortly outgrow

it. That is, if those sharp little teeth haven't chewed the basket to shreds first.

My recommendation would be to invest in a wire or fiberglass crate for your puppy (see Crate Training, page 29). Line the crate with a washable mat or throw rug. Or you might want to purchase a cedar-chip filled pillow with a washable, removable cover. The key here is "washable." The dalmatian has short, straight hair that it sheds frequently.

## Keeping Your Dalmatian Outdoors

A dalmatian is very comfortable in the out-of-doors. It can adapt to somewhat lower temperatures better than it can adapt to high heat and humidity. If you have a fenced-in yard, an outdoor kennel can be a cozy home for your pet. It can run, play with the family kittens, or chase its own shadow. Having its own yard, its own doghouse, all contribute to a healthy, happy life-style. It's also no

A well-planned doghouse: floor raised off the ground for temperature and humidity control, slanted roof to shed rain and snow, and draft-free bedroom.

small advantage that it is much easier to house-break a dalmatian that primarily lives outside.

If yours is an outdoor dalmatian, it will need protection from weather extremes. Its outdoor kennel house should be out of the flow of yard traffic and sheltered from winter winds and driving spring rains. The kennel should be raised somewhat off the ground for extra comfort in summer. Make provisions to add some heat to the kennel for cold winter nights, too. A dalmatian's short coat doesn't offer much protection against freezing temperatures.

Position the entrance of the kennel so your puppy can watch for you. You will find that your dalmatian will spend a great deal of time facing the back door or the side gate or wherever you first appear. So turn its door to face that side if you can. Some people put windows in their dog's house. Why not? It's nice to be able to see out.

**An Outside Run:** If you can't fence in your entire yard, why not build an outside run, enclosing a kennel house? A wire fence 8 feet (2.4 m) wide and 16 feet (5 m) long should give a dalmatian plenty of exercise room until you can take it out on a leash. Economical runs of 11 gauge wire can be constructed by the home owner handyman. Pet

This contented, well cared for dalmatian has its own house and yard.

shops and catalogs also carry ready-made runs you might like to look at. Any of these runs can be adapted easily to your backyard.

## Exercise

This reminder is particularly important for indoor dalmatians. Your dal requires plenty of exercise. Take it with you on a leash when you bike. As often as possible, take your puppy on a leash for a fast walk in the park. Take it to the country where it can run free. Spend 20 minutes playing catch and fetch.

Even if your dalmatian lives out-of-doors, it would appreciate an opportunity to run with you.

Do remember, though, to use moderation when exercising your puppy. Because of the fact that a dalmatian is still part puppy at one year of age, letting it run on hard surfaces for more than 20 minutes at a stretch is not a good idea. The puppy's skeletal and muscular structures are still forming. The constant stress and pounding on its joints can lead to complications later. Because your puppy is eager to do what you ask, it may not realize it is being hurt. As in other areas of the puppy's life, you must think for both of you.

It is difficult to tire an adult dalmatian. That brisk trot has been bred into it. After so many years of following the horses, it can maintain a steady pace for hours.

Even though your dalmatian has a yard to play in, take it out occasionally for a run across an open field. Only exercise will develop the dalmatian's muscles into the long, lean, elegant shape we love. If yours is a city dalmatian, and trained to heel, try bicycling alongside your pet. You'll tire before your dalmatian does. Both of you will have better circulation and better breathing habits than before you started out.

Exercising your dal can be as simple as playing. Bend down and clap your knees. Your puppy soon will recognize the signal and come running.

A solid rubber ball (one impossible for the puppy to swallow) set to rolling will send a frisky

# *Living with Your Dalmatian*

This dal would be an asset to any volleyball team unless those sharp teeth puncture the ball.

dalmatian into a frenzy. A final pounce gets the ball under control.

It's best not to let anyone play tug-of-war with your dalmatian. It doesn't need the jaw activity. The game may loosen teeth that should stay in place awhile longer. It teaches bad habits.

**Find It:** "Find it" is a wonderful game that can keep a dog active for longer than you probably want to play. A dalmatian has a very discriminating nose. And a dalmatian loves treats. Put these factors together.

Put your dal in a "sit/stay." Hold a dog biscuit or piece of liver at eye level. Say, "smell it!" Don't let the dog grab the treat. Now place the treat on the ground beside you and say, "find it!" Of course, your dog will go right for it. Praise as if your dog had succeeded beyond your wildest dreams.

The secret to this game is gradual escalation. Use a variety of rewards for bait. Gradually increase the difficulty of the hunt. When you think your dal understands "find it," switch to a ball, or a dumbbell, or a favorite toy. At this stage of the training, always give a real treat along with hearty praise. Next time, put the object on a higher level, a step for instance, instead of on the floor. Then move the search to another room. Hide the object instead of leaving it in plain sight.

Don't start this game before six months of age. Be patient. Your dalmatian will learn as soon as it understands. You'll both have a lot of fun.

**Jump:** Dalmatians love to jump. You knew that when your dal was a puppy, didn't you?

It should be easy to teach your puppy to jump over a low hurdle and return to you. Start small. If you feed the puppy in the laundry room, place a 1-foot (30 cm) high board in the doorway. When the puppy wants to get into its room, it will jump over the board. If the puppy is hesitant, jump over with it.

If the puppy still hesitates, put its leash on. Stand on one side of the board and call your dog by name in your friendliest voice, "Dotty, come." As the puppy nears the board call, "over," and pull on the leash. Praise extravagantly when the puppy gets to you.

A dalmatian usually can jump at least one and one half times its height at the shoulder. This means an adult dalmatian can be trained to jump 3 feet (.9 m) or more.

**Fetch:** Retrieving is a good game that most dalmatians handle very well. "Fetch" takes patience. Don't expect consistent results until your dal is at least six months old.

This game is best learned indoors. Find some soft, friendly toy like a knotted sock. Dangle the toy in front of your puppy. Then toss the toy a couple of feet. Say "fetch!" The puppy will head out. Praise lavishly. Give the puppy a lot of encouragement. Sure, the going out is the easy part. You know that. Getting the sock back is the trick.

If your dog runs off with the toy, or settles down to nibble on it, do whatever you can to get both the dog and toy back. If you move forward to take the toy and the puppy runs off with it, don't chase. This is why we started this game indoors. The puppy can't run far. Go in the other direction. Call the puppy. When it comes, with or without the toy, use praise. If the puppy seems interested, go and get the toy and try again.

"Fetch" works eventually because the dog figures out that if you don't have the toy, it doesn't get to play anymore. After the dog consistently returns the toy to you, graduate to outside. At that point, you can change to a ball, a dowel, or a rolled up newspaper.

## Dalmatians and Children

Dalmatians like children. They are especially devoted to children who are members of their own pack. Children age seven and older can learn to respond appropriately to this affection. Teach a young child to sit down to pet the dog. If a new child comes into the yard, be on hand for the introduction. If the youngster is scared, stand by. Do your best not to let the child run away. Running only turns a fascinating game into a contest the dog invariably wins.

Do you have a baby? Was the dog there first? Some owners try to keep the dog and baby separated. Usually the dog is not fooled. It knows someone else is around.

Most authorities suggest that unless you have good reason not to, you should introduce the baby and the dog. Stand over the two while both of them sniff and smell and touch. This applies, of course, to dogs that you have trained and are confident of. Don't give your dalmatian any grounds for jealousy. Your dog must understand that the baby is also a member of the pack.

## Naming Your Dal

One decision that can wait awhile is what to name your puppy. Sometimes we have to see a dog before we know what we can call it. We have to live

with it for a little while, observe the puppy in action.

You probably will want to take a look at the puppy's pedigree. See if any family names strike your fancy. Dalmatians are courtly, gentle dogs. Many bear titles of ancient royalty, their names preceded by Count or Prince. Some dalmatians are given names suggesting their history, as Gipsy, Stallions, Fortune Teller, and Joker. Other names focus on the dalmatian's unique coloration.

One delightfully inventive owner named her puppy Cyclops, a choice obvious to all who saw the big spot in the middle of his forehead. Another thought Spuds, in recognition of a famous advertising personality, appropriate for her dalmatian. Speckles, Smoky, and Sparky are friends of mine. Freckles, Bandit, and Pepper are waiting for you.

The perky little dalmatian that is the subject of this book has a name, too. It isn't original, but it suits everybody just fine. We call our dalmatian Dotty.

## Special Circumstances

Most of our day-to-day activities are close to home. Occasionally, though, we are faced with a situation that needs special handling. Traveling with your dal and boarding it when you must, are two situations that can strain our resources.

In today's busy world we must all be travel-wise. If your dog can accompany you on a trip, you need to be prepared with travel bowls and bedding. If your pet must stay behind for a few days, it's helpful to have a few other tricks up your sleeve.

### Traveling with Your Dal

If you have a dog, you're going to have to put it in the car at some point, if only for a visit to the veterinarian. It stands to reason that if your dal is a good traveler, you'll be a lot happier on the road. Set up a travel kennel in the back seat. Add a chew toy. Put your dog in it. Any other solution ends with the dog jumping onto your lap, smearing the win-

# Living with Your Dalmatian

dows, and perhaps getting carsick on you or your passengers.

Do whatever you can to make the first car trips fun. Take short trips. Go to a fun place like a park or to the country. Don't leave right after a meal. Carry a thermos of cold water with you. When you stop for a rest, give your dal a break, too.

On trips of several days, bring your dog's feeding dish, a supply of its favorite food, and a list of hotels and motels that accept pets. When you stop for lunch or to sightsee, you can park the car in the shade and open all the windows!

Make sure your pet's vaccinations are up-to-date. Be sure your name and phone number are on its collar.

**The Car—Summer's Death Trap:** Remember that the interior of a closed car, even one parked in the shade, can turn into an oven in a few minutes. One rule of thumb is, ask yourself if you would stay in the car under those conditions. Then decide if you will leave your pet.

**Air Travel:** Today we often find ourselves miles from a new job. If the choice is to ship our dal or leave it behind, there is no choice. Carefully planned air travel is no more a hardship on your dalmatian than it is on you or the children. In this instance, having a pet accustomed to a dog crate is a blessing.

The basic rules are simple. Have your pet's shots up to date. If you are leaving the country, be sure to check the licensing and quarantine regulations long before you leave. Some countries do not permit dogs to enter without a six-month quarantine period. Carry your dal's veterinarian records and health certificate on your person, not in your luggage.

Your pet will travel in the cargo space. Make its reservation when you make yours. Don't feed your dog within six to eight hours of a flight. Bring bowls, food, and water in your carryon. Be ready to feed and exercise your pet at your destination.

## Boarding Your Dalmatian

Most veterinarians offer kennels at a reasonable cost. The staff, composed of conscientious animal lovers, will welcome your pet as an old friend. You might use this time to have your dal checked for parasites, have its nails clipped, or have it bathed.

Be sure to bring all the daily necessities: food, feeding dish, favorite toys, vitamins.

# *Diet*

## A Word on Animal Nutrition

Earlier, we named five basic items that will make a puppy feel loved. Food and water were at the top of the list. (A bed of its own, a chew toy, and *you* were the others.) For your dog's continuing health, from a puppy through old age, it is important that you feed it properly. Proper feeding doesn't necessarily mean you have to become an instant nutritionist. It doesn't mean you must spend a lot of money on your dog's diet. Nor does it mean spending hours at the grocery analyzing bag contents. Well-qualified animal specialists have researched this part for you already.

What proper feeding does mean is proper management of your dal's nutritional needs at different stages of its life. A puppy, an older dog, a pregnant or nursing female, an overweight dog, or a dalmatian with bladder stones, do not have the same feeding requirements. It is up to you to provide the proper diet in the proper amounts.

Some protein, plenty of carbohydrates, and fat are essential to every dog's health. The proportion of these valuable nutrients that our dog requires changes with its age and life-style. As we have learned more about a dog's needs at different stages of its life, our ideas about how to obtain these necessary nutrients have changed, too.

## Protein

All dogs require top quality proteins for good growth and development. The amount required varies with the dog's life-style and age. Puppies, for example, need twice as much protein than grown dogs. In a dal, inadequate protein levels will result in a dull coat, and eventually, loss of hair.

Animal owners used to believe that a healthy dog needed meat proteins. Today, however, we have learned that red meat is not essential for a well-balanced canine diet. A dog can get quality protein from chicken, fish, cheese, and cereals, such as oats and brown rice. As a matter of fact, dogs in some parts of the world make substantial meals off of whole cooked fish.

## Carbohydrates

Most commercial preparations do a good job of providing carbohydrates. These starches and sugars are the foundation of your dog's health and energy balance. A dog that does not receive enough carbohydrates from its diet automatically will convert proteins to carbohydrates. This loss can create protein deficiencies. If you suspect that your dog needs more carbohydrates, try adding mashed potatoes, boiled rice, or cooked cereals to its diet.

## Fats

Nutritionists recommend that fats and fatty foods make up at least 20 percent of a dog's diet. Read the label on your commercially prepared food. A dalmatian fed only dry dog food could be getting insufficient fat. Many dal owners add 1 or 2 teaspoons (5–10 ml) of gravy, melted chicken fat, or bacon grease to their pet's daily ration of dry food.

## Bones, Dog Biscuits, Hide Bones

Dogs love bones. Thick, sturdy beef bones, carried off to enjoy privately, are a treat for your pet and no problem for you. You and your dog would be well off if you provided beef bones and threw fish, chicken, pork, veal, or rabbit bones into the trash. The major danger in feeding these brittle, snappy bones is the chance that a sliver will lodge in your dog's mouth or throat. If your dog does bolt a fish bone and seems all right afterward, don't worry. Once the bone passes into the stomach, powerful gastric juices soften it in less than an hour.

Dog biscuits should be used as treats, sparingly. These "baked starch" snacks are at the bottom of the nutritional charts. When fed in large amounts, dog biscuits can even be constipating to some dogs. If your dog has a tendency to be overweight, be sure to note and keep track of the biscuit's calorie content and add it to the day's total.

Although most dogs love rawhide chews, many veterinarians do not recommend them for adult dogs. When the rawhide softens, the dog tears off and swallows large chunks. Rawhide strips lodged in the intestine can cause a blockage. The chews are all right for puppies. Some owners would say chews are a necessity.

A sterilized cow hoof chew now on the market is popular with veterinarians, owners, and dogs. As in all things important to the health of your dalmatian, ask your veterinarian or pet supply source for suggestions.

## Types of Food

Studies have shown that dogs can eat what humans eat. Dog owners used to say, "Don't feed a dog potatoes," for instance. This is because chunks of potatoes are as indigestible to your dog as whole kernels of corn are to you. Potatoes are a wholesome carbohydrate. Just be sure to mash or break potatoes up into small pieces before adding them to the dog's supper.

This suggestion holds true for many types of food. Because dogs "bolt" their food, without making any pretense of chewing, you should break large chunks of meat, for instance, into manageable bits first.

## Homemade

The old debate between homemade and commercial food takes place less and less often these days. In today's busy households, few families have time to make up their own dog food. Several veterinary books offer complete directions and analyses for homemade mixes if you still are inclined. And if you do decide to take the dog's nutrition into your own hands, you should invest in one of these books. Some of the following suggestions from home feeding programs have merit.

Feed your puppy a diet containing about 30 percent protein, 20 percent fat, and the rest, carbohydrates. For an adult dog, the protein can be reduced to 20 to 25 percent, fats can stay at 20 percent and carbohydrates can take up the balance.

For protein, you may use fresh, lean, raw meat from the muscle or heart or liver. You may mix it with chicken, fish, or cottage cheese.

For carbohydrates, add boiling grains, such as rice, oats, or cornmeal. Mix with such cooked vegetables as beans, peas, or corn. Commercial preparations do not need vitamin supplementation. In fact, supplementation might be harmful because you could upset a carefully balanced program. You should, however, supplement the homemade diet with a commercial vitamin preparation recommended by your veterinarian.

**Table Scraps:** Feeding leftovers is one way we can feed our dogs a commercial diet and still vary the contents. In fact, some leftovers can be an excellent addition to your dog's diet. Not too many, though. A steady diet of table scraps isn't good for your friend.

To feed, transfer the scraps to the puppy's own dish, mixing leftovers in with its regular diet. Don't give your dalmatian leftover fried foods. Stop short at dessert. Make cake and candies a very rare treat. All chocolates and all pies are off-limits.

## Commercial

Commercial pet food manufacturers spend enormous amounts of money on nutritional research. This research assures the consumer of a quality product. Extensive feeding trials by these major manufacturers have taught us much about our own nutritional needs.

You will find that the same manufacturer usually offers food at three levels of preparedness: dry, semimoist, and canned. The choice usually is dictated by your personal preference and the size of the dog.

**Read the Label:** As part of the pet food regulations adopted by the Association of American Feed Control Officials, a list of ingredients is on all pet food packages. An analysis on the label includes information about the amount of fat, protein, fiber, and other materials in the product.

In general, the major manufacturers offer a well-balanced and reliable product. Those dog foods sold through veterinarians and pet supply shops usually contain fewer indigestible fibers with higher quality control. The best products result in a moderately low output: few, firm stools. If you decide to try a grocery store brand, watch your dog's stool for a few weeks. Poor quality protein and too much indigestible filler result in watery, mushy, foamy stools.

**Dry:** Usually called "complete" foods, dry kibbles are half cereal and half animal in origin. Although some kibbles sold by veterinarians and pet supply stores contain up to 17 percent fat, the fat content of other brands is rarely as high as 10 percent.

Dry kibble collects mold when damp. Try to purchase your supply from a source with a fast moving stock. When you get home, store the sack in a dry place. Don't feed your pet molded food. Throw it out.

If you open a buggy bag of dry food, or a buggy box of bones, ask the merchant to replace it. If your food is special order and you can't get a new bag quickly, a few bugs in dry kibble will not hurt your dog. You will find, however, that the bugs will transfer to other items in your storage area. Again, buy a reliable product from a reputable source.

**Canned:** At about 450 calories, each regular size can of dog food contains about enough daily ration for one 15-pound (7 kg) dog. For an active, 45-pound (20 kg) dalmatian, that works out to about three cans of food each day. These canned products, about 78 percent water, pour out with the consistency of a thick soup or pudding. Although the canned dog food products have an impressive smell, often they contain less protein and less fat than the poorer kibbles. Read the label.

**Semimoist:** Semimoist dog food is packaged in small cellophane wrapped pouches. The product in these serving size containers is colored to resemble ground hamburger or chunks of stew meat. The moisture content is around 35 percent. The packages lack the odor of canned food, are lightweight, and are useful on a trip. They take little storage room, need no refrigeration, and can be served quickly. Like canned food, this product is an expensive steady diet for a grown dalmatian.

Recommending exactly how much to feed your pet each day is a difficult task. Each animal should be fed according to its needs. Nutritional needs are based on the amount of physical activity your pet receives, the "extras" you feed it, and its metabolism. The best test is to look at your dog. Does it look fat? Stand over the dog. You can feel a healthy dog's ribs. Watch your dog move. Is is sluggish or is it alert? It is much easier to keep your dalmatian from getting fat than to put it on a diet.

## Special Diets

Puppies have special nutritional needs. Most dog food manufacturers provide enhanced diets to meet these requirements. Likewise, if your dalmatian is overweight, has a tendency to kidney and bladder stones, or is advanced in age, it most likely will require a special diet. Your veterinarian will give you details.

### Puppies Under Five Months Old

Veterinarians usually say to "feed the puppy up to its appetite." This means feed the puppy if not all it wants, at least all it can eat without an upset stomach. Remember also that a puppy must not go more than eight hours without food.

A dalmatian usually will double its birth weight in two to three weeks. A weaning dalmatian (four to six weeks old) should be fed five or six times a day. From three to five months old, feed your puppy at least four times a day: early morning, mid-morning, mid-afternoon and supper time.

Puppies require twice as much protein and 50 percent more calories than adult dogs. Be careful not to overdo the vitamins and extras. Your puppy

# *Diet*

Mealtime can help forge a close bond between you and your dalmatian. Be consistent. Feed every meal at the same time and in the same place.

could grow too fast and develop skeletal problems later. Dog foods specifically are formulated to take care of a puppy's special needs. Don't disturb the balance.

When you do add foods to the puppy's diet, remember that raw meat is digested more easily than cooked meat. Egg yolks, raw or cooked, are excellent. Avoid giving your dog raw egg whites.

## Puppies Five to Twelve Months Old

By the time the puppy is five months old, feedings can be reduced to three times a day: morning, noon, and evening. By six or seven months, cut meal times to twice a day. Feed your dog as much as it will eat in 20 minutes. As always, feed whatever amount will keep your dalmatian lean. Carrying too much weight is as serious a health problem in dogs as in people.

## Adult Dalmatians

An adult dalmatian may be fed once a day. You might like to consider a self-feeder bin. Food is kept dry and fresh and before the dog at all times.

Owners agree that most self-fed dogs do not overeat. For some dalmatians, five months and older, the self-feeder is a perfect solution. But you should take a good look at your dalmatian's eating habits before you purchase a self-feeder and talk to your veterinarian before you make the investment.

Your dog needs a steady supply of fresh, cool water, especially in the summer. The automatic pet watering dish is an innovation pet owners and their charges appreciate. The water basin, connected to an outside faucet, automatically refills when the water drops below a certain level. It requires little care except a daily clean out of leaves and debris.

## Pregnant and Lactating Dalmatians

If your pregnant dalmatian is on one of the modern, well-balanced dog foods, her diet probably won't need supplementing. Occasionally, for a treat, you might want to add extra protein to her supper dish. Try evaporated milk, scrambled eggs, cottage cheese, or raw liver. Some breeders recommend switching her to a puppy chow formula of the same brand she already is accustomed to. Puppy formulas are higher in protein, which is beneficial for pregnant and nursing bitches. If you do switch, keep her on it until the litter is weaned.

A nursing dalmatian will require three times the calories she ordinarily would consume. Otherwise she will lose weight and will not produce the milk necessary to feed her litter.

## The Ailing Dalmatian

The dalmatian is one of the breeds most susceptible to bladder and kidney stones. If your dalmatian is affected, a special prescription diet, low in minerals and protein, may be prescribed by your veterinarian.

## The Aged Dalmatian

At this time in a dog's life, certain modifications to its diet probably will be necessary. As a dog gets older, it is less active and usually does better on less food. Now don't be too quick about this.

# *Diet*

Observe your dog. If it is accustomed to eating once a day, and has no weight problem, leave well enough alone. If your dalmatian seems to be having digestive problems, though, or leaves some of its food and comes back later acting hungry, try switching to twice a day feedings to see if that helps.

## The Finicky Eater

Dalmatians are not ordinarily fussy eaters. If, from the beginning, you feed your dalmatian a high-quality kibble, with occasional added treats, it will eat heartily all its life.

We cause finicky eaters by presuming a dog should eat what we eat. A lot of what we eat isn't even good for our pets. You shouldn't give your dog fried potatoes, pie, or chocolate candy, for instance. It is better to train our pets to eat what we set before them. A puppy reared on a diet of dry kibble will enjoy every bite. People think the dog may get tired of that same old diet. It does not. A dog can taste all the flavors in a kibble. Just try to add a little pill to a bowl of dry dog food and see what's left rolling around when the dog has finished.

If you already have let your dog get particular about what it eats, try an experiment. Mix some of whatever it loves with whatever you want to change it to. Go slow. Don't be too quick to give up. Let your dog miss a meal or two until it gets hungry. Although I don't subscribe to the theory that fasting once a month or once a week is good for a dog because "that's how dogs in the wild live," I don't think your pet will starve while you are accustoming it to what you want to serve. There are recorded instances of dogs living on nothing but water for two months.

## Food Fallacies

Some of the old tales that have been handed down through the years make no sense in the light of today's nutritional knowledge.

*Milk makes worms.* Research shows that milk is as good for dogs as meat. Buttermilk often settles an ill dog's stomach by restoring healthy bacteria.

*Garlic gets rid of worms and fleas.* We can find no evidence that garlic destroys internal or external parasites. Although some pet owners swear by brewer's yeast and garlic, neither additive has been proven clinically to be of any benefit.

*Potatoes are indigestible and can give the dog a rash.* It is true that large lumps of potatoes pass through the dog almost undigested. But the key words are "large" and "lumps." Mashing a potato to break it into smaller pieces is the solution.

## Food Economies

Studies show that dry food is the most economical. Canned and semimoist cost about twice as much as the best kibbles. If you plan to feed your dal homemade food, plan to spend six times as much as for a quality dehydrated kibble.

## Begging

Some people feed scraps directly from the table. This may be your choice in the beginning because up on two hind legs that spotted little puppy does look appealing and cute, but table begging doesn't usually work out. Besides the fact that the dog can be a nuisance when you have company, begging can be a distraction to other family members.

# Training Your Dalmatian

## What Is Obedience Training?

Obedience Training is nothing more or less than teaching a dog to behave. A well-behaved dog doesn't chase cars, jump on guests, bark all night, or bite the delivery person. An untrained dog is a nuisance. It is a problem to you and your neighbors. Untrained dogs are responsible for the bad press many breeds are receiving.

My mother told a story one time about a lady neighbor whose children had beautiful manners. Even the two-year-old was pleasant and well behaved. Someone asked the mother what her secret was. I'll never forget the answer. "If something ever happens to me," the lady replied, "that I couldn't take care of them, I would want to know that somebody would step up and say, 'What lovely children. I'd be delighted to bring them home with me.'"

In parts of Europe, owners are held responsible for the actions of their pets. Their dogs, if well behaved, are welcome in stores, in bars and restaurants, in parks, and on the beaches. Many American communities, on the other hand, strictly prohibit dogs from these places. These communities usually require more than up-to-date license tags and owner responsibility. Many neighborhood parks, state and national parks, recreation areas, and controlled subdivisions will not allow a dog on the premises unless it is restrained by a leash no longer than 6-feet (1.8 m). Some breeds are outlawed altogether, which is a sad development for responsible owners and their pets.

Obedience training your dalmatian is a matter of mutual self-discipline. Your dog should learn to obey you instantly with one and only one command. You should learn not to give a command that can be disobeyed.

Some dog lovers say that they are satisfied if their dog responds to only two instructions: "come" and "no." Surely both of these commands can make your life, and your dalmatian's life, better. A dalmatian that comes when it is called is terrific. One that stops digging in the garbage or stops barking on a "no" command deserves high praise. A dalmatian that drops on command and is saved from running into the path of a speeding truck, is obedience trained.

## Before You Begin

Each dalmatian is different in temperament, intelligence, and aptitude. Although a dalmatian is best trained by gentle, positive persuasion, there is no one way to train. In the first place, one dalmatian will respond in two different ways to two different handlers. Successful trainers, amateur and professional, are those who recognize a dog's tendencies and work within them.

If you have observed your dalmatian long enough to have a clear insight into its temperament and its abilities, your job as trainer is half done. If that same dalmatian is alert to your moods, enjoys playtime, and anticipates your actions, training time will be a pleasure for both of you.

## How Often Can We Work?

Serious obedience training should wait until your dalmatian is at least seven months old. Before that time, the dog's ability to concentrate will be handicapped. It will be drawn off course by stray leaves, unusual smells, and its own tail.

Dogs are creatures of habit. Trainers, keeping in mind the dog's tendencies, follow set guidelines.
- Work at the same times every day. Just before mealtime is great. A good meal can be a reward of its own.
- Hold sessions twice a day, for not longer than 15 to 20 minutes each time.
- Let one person be the trainer. Other family members can be the support team, but the puppy should have one master.
- Don't work if you're in a bad mood.
- Follow each session with ten minutes of playtime.

# *Training Your Dalmatian*

## Corrections and Rewards

One of the most important points to remember is that both rewards and correction should be given immediately. They have been a puppy's way of life since it was in the kennel. The mother licked it when it was good and growled when she taught a lesson. The puppy grew up expecting guidelines. It will respond to them promptly.

When you are working with your dog, treat it as you would a child. Correct with love. Don't be harsh, don't be impatient, don't expect miracles. Be firm. A disgusted voice can be discipline enough. And do persevere. Once you start a lesson, keep repeating it until the dog understands.

## Food Training, Yes or No?

Some trainers swear by food as a reward. Others insist love and discipline are all that are necessary. Judging from recent literature, food trainers are winning the day. Let's see why.

First, most dogs adore training food. Treats, such as dog biscuits or boiled liver, are a highlight in their day. Food becomes a positive motivation. A dog learns to interact between an activity on its part and reward.

Second, in a limited way, dogs can think. If you hold up a piece of food, or reach for the treat jar, a smart dog will sit in front of you and try to anticipate what it is you want it to do.

Third, dalmatians particularly enjoy showing off their skills. Some would be happy earning all their food. They like being useful and they love your praise.

And last, a smart dalmatian likes knowing what the score is. Plus it wants your approval. Its outlook on life, its confidence, is developed by the disciplined way in which you handle its training.

## Your Training Tools

A dog has a simple mind. If you and your dal have the right relationship, it will obey you when it understands what you want of it. It is up to you to make it clear to the dog what you want.

Use as few words as possible—one word is best. Don't say "okay" one time, for instance, and "good" later. Don't say "down" for get off the sofa or quit jumping and then "down" for lie down.

Your goal is to give the command only once. During training, of course, you will need to repeat the commands several times.

## Collar and Lead

Your puppy already has a collar and leash. By the time your puppy is six or seven months old, you should purchase a metal training collar, known as a choke chain. The important thing to remember is that the purpose of the collar is to get your dog's attention. Collared and corrected properly, the dog does not choke. When you are using the collar, it lies high on the dog's neck, just behind the ears.

The trick to putting on a choke chain is sometimes difficult to master. Try holding one ring of the chain in the thumb and index finger of your left hand. Attach the lead to the ring in your right hand. Then thread the chain (with the lead attached) through the empty ring. Face the dog. Put the chain on the dog so that the ring with the lead attached lies counterclockwise over the dog's neck. The leash is on the left of the ring as you face it. A swift correction will tighten the collar. When you release the pressure, the collar immediately hangs free.

## The Right Tone of Voice

Your voice and your body language are both important training tools. The right tone of voice, in fact, is critical. Do your best to cultivate two different tones, a praise and a correction voice. If

Training should be a positive experience for you and your ►
dal. "Shake" (or "Paw") is fun, but far less important than "Heel," "Stay," and the other basics. Teaching your dal to release a splintery stick or other potentially dangerous object is another important lesson.

# *Training Your Dalmatian*

your everyday voice is naturally high pitched, try using a low, commanding voice when you give a correction. Put some authority into your voice. A dalmatian can be stubborn. You may have to correct often for the same thing. Don't get angry, just be firm. Be stubborn yourself. Don't give up the leadership.

Now, adopt a happy, loving, singsong voice for praise. Watch trainers at work and in the show ring (still at work). A good trainer can make a puppy feel like it is the sweetest, brightest, best behaved dog ever born. That puppy will follow that person anywhere, do anything it understands how to do, to hear that voice again. And here is the most important point: remember that this loving, singsong praise voice follows right on the heels of the low, stern correction voice.

Once your training voices are in place, don't forget to talk to the dog with your body, too. If necessary, jump up and down, applaud and throw your arms around the dog when giving praise. When you give a correction to your dog, be stiff. Stand erect, then turn away, and avert your eyes.

## The Basic Obedience Commands

Actually, by the time your puppy is three months old, it already has learned one command, "no!" If you followed the suggestions given in First Lessons (see page 21), your dalmatian is familiar with "sit," too.

One reminder: The moving commands ("come" and "heel"), are preceded by your dog's name. When you want your puppy to obey a stationary command, ("sit," "stay," and "down"), omit its name.

Each of these commands is begun on a leash. We have said how important it is not to let your dog disobey a command. Don't try these commands off a leash until you are very confident you can make your dog obey them. If you do go off the leash and the dog even looks like it isn't going to obey, step in right away. Catch the dog before it has a chance to do otherwise. Give the command again, and go back to leash training if necessary.

A dog should obey a command until released. To release, tell your puppy "okay." Then give it a pat, a treat, and a rousing round of praise. Play with your dog. Put on your most friendly voice and tell it what a good puppy it is.

## Sit

"Sit" is known as the attention-getting command. Actually, "sit" is one of the easiest commands for your dalmatian to learn. As a puppy, your dal learned to sit for supper, for a heartworm tablet, for a treat. Because "sit" is so useful, and so easy to teach, many owners use it as the basis of any training.

The command "sit." Apply upward pressure on the leash in your right hand as you push down on your dal's hindquarters with your left hand.

Learn to understand your dal's facial expressions, vocalizations, and body language. The "smarl," a tight-lipped smile, is a distinctive dal characteristic.

If you did not teach your puppy to "sit" at mealtime, work on it now. Put your dal on your left side, on a leash. Hold the leash in your right hand. Do not use your dog's name. Command "sit." Pull up on the leash and push down on the dog's hindquarters with your left hand. The dog will sit. Praise it. This command is very easy for the dog to remember. It is easy to practice. You will be pleased at how fast your dog learns.

Within a day or two, you won't have to push down on the dog. Then your left hand will be free to give the hand signal with the verbal command. Hold your left hand stiffly in front of your dog's face, fingers up. Say "sit."

"Sit" is also a part of heeling. The dog is expected to sit (at the handler's left side), facing straight ahead, whenever the handler stops moving.

## Come

"Come" is called the command that must be obeyed. This command is preceded by your dog's name. Most trainers teach "come" on a leash, after putting the dog in a sitting position. Don't try "come" off the lead, and don't command "come" unless you are very sure the dog will obey you. If you let your puppy know it can disobey, you have a long road ahead of you.

Because of its importance, you should make the invitation to "come" attractive. Get down and play with your dal when it comes. Give it a treat and a hug. Make your dog glad it came to you instead of chasing that scent that almost lured it away.

Instead of a hand signal, many trainers use a whistle for "come." The signal is a trill—beep-beep-beep, not a single blast. A young dal in the field has many distractions. You don't want to come in second. In training, start calling or whistling immediately after you shout the command and continue the whole time the dog is coming to you. Its instincts tell it to look toward you to be sure the command hasn't changed.

Because it is so important that your dog obey "come," you should avoid two prime errors. First, don't ever ignore a dog who has obeyed this command. Praise the dog, no matter how long it took to come. Put on your happy voice even if the dog took ten minutes and you had to blow your whistle every step of the way.

Second, never correct or discipline your dog after you have called it to you. In the dog's mind, it obeyed the last command. It will not understand a correction. If you have to, go back to training on a leash. Again, you want to be sure the dog understands. The problem arises when the dog does understand and still wants to play king of the hill with you. You must be sure you stay the boss. Don't give in and agree that it's a beautiful spring day and you wouldn't want to return, either. When your stray spotted friend returns, welcome it. But be ready to do some leash work as a reminder that you are still the leader of the pack.

## Heel

With the dog on your left side, call your dog by name, "Dotty, heel!" Step off on your left foot (the foot closest to your puppy). Give a light jerk on the lead. As you walk, keep a short lead. Walk in a straight line. Don't let your dog's attention wander. Keep up a stream of talk and praise. Use your special praise voice. "What a good dog! That's a good puppy! Dotty's a good dog! Look at us go. Let's go, Dotty. Here we go! Good girl!" You have the leash. Your dog will follow. The combination of a short lead and a loving voice are irresistible. Its first lesson was a success. Praise, praise, praise.

Later, you can change course. Stop, reverse. The same principles apply to all. Keep your dog's attention. When you have to correct, do so with a swift jerk on the lead. Give your dog no option. Then praise it for obeying. The mildly uncomfortable correction gets the dog's attention. The praise is music to its ears.

Practice heeling on a lead until the two of you can move in circles, around corners, and among other dogs without having to give or receive a

# *Training Your Dalmatian*

When at "heel," keep your puppy's attention focused on you. Talk to it. Pat your leg. Change directions.

correction. You might try a little body language. Pat your leg as a signal that you're going to turn, and lean a little in the direction of the turn.

## Stay

Once you are sure your dalmatian is familiar with "sit," "come," and "heel," move on to "stay." This is a very important command and has a number of uses. Perhaps you want to walk across the street for a minute. You don't want your dog to follow. Perhaps on the way home from a bicycle outing, you want to stop at the grocery store. You have to leave the dog and bike outside. Here's how.

First, put the puppy on a leash in a sit position at your left foot, facing forward. Command "stay." Put your left hand in front of the puppy's nose (even touching the muzzle at first). This time, your fingers are pointing down. Step off on your right foot. Which foot you use is very important because

you have already trained your puppy to identify a *left* foot start with the "heel" command.

Now, take one or at most two steps away. Keep your hands on your dog, if necessary to keep it from following. Watch carefully and be ready to correct immediately at the first hint of movement. Keep the stay short—under 30 seconds at first. Say "okay" and give you dog a lot of praise.

When you are sure your dog won't break on a short stay, vary the lessons. Try going to the end of the leash. Try a 12-foot (3.7 m) leash. Try a longer stay. Try going out of sight for a minute. Again, watch carefully. Be ready to jump back. Your dog will want to follow you. Don't let it move. Stand at the end of a 6-foot (1.8 m) leash. Say "stay," and tug on the leash. Really pull hard. Your dog should tug back. Say "okay," and praise.

A well-trained dalmatian will hold a "sit/stay" for three minutes, even if its master is out of sight.

# *Training Your Dalmatian*

When your dog holds this stay, try a "stay" off the leash. This is a very hard command because your dog's instincts are to follow you. Be ready to go back on the leash at the first sign of disobedience.

## Down

"Down" is really an optional command. It shouldn't be taught with other commands. Don't say a word about "down," for instance, until your puppy is letter-perfect on "sit." It shouldn't be used to stop jumping or get off the sofa. The command for "get your feet off the counter" is "no." "Down" means "lie down."

To teach "down," don't use the dog's name. Put your dal on a leash. Give the "sit" command. Then, very deliberately and slowly, say "down." Put your foot on the leash and pull down. If necessary, put your arm over the puppy's back and take hold of its left leg with your left hand. Take hold of the puppy's right leg with your right hand. Say "down" again. Keep the dog down for 30 seconds. Release your pressure and then praise and treat. Repeat as often as necessary until the dog will go down without any pressure at all.

## Stand

A "stand" is very useful for veterinary examinations. A "stand-stay" is required for judge's examinations at shows.

Put your dog on your left in the "sitting at heel" position. Hold the leash in your right hand. Put your right hand and leash in front of the dog's nose. Command "stand." Reach over and tickle the dog's stomach with your left hand. Pull up on the leash with your right hand. Praise your dog.

If you're having trouble getting your point across, make a loop in the leash and place it around the puppy's stomach. Command "stand" and pull up on the lead. The puppy won't learn "stand" as quickly as it learned "sit," but it'll get there. Don't forget. Even if you had to do all the work, praise your dog.

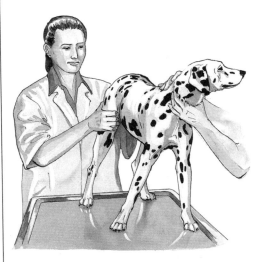

The command "stand" is useful for veterinary examinations and in the show ring.

## Training Problems

Correct sloppy, unreliable responses immediately. If you have to repeat a command, if Dotty takes her good old time coming to you, or worse, doesn't come at all, it's time for some extra work.

Go back at least one step. If necessary, go back to leash training. Be firm. Look your dog in the eye. (Don't break first on this one.)

### Unrealistic Expectations

Seasoned trainers don't expect perfection from a puppy until it is at least one year old. This doesn't mean that a well-trained puppy can't earn a companion dog degree at seven months. Many have. It just means that the average owner handled family dalmatian often has other things to think about. It wonders where that cat went off to and where squirrels go when they disappear. We had one country dog that sniffed and scratched around the bottom of a tree for five minutes and never in his life learned to look up in the branches.

## AKC Obedience Trial Regulations

For those of you who would like to go further down the training path, and whose dalmatian is willing, following are the basic regulations for AKC Obedience Trials. A complete set of rules may be obtained by writing to the American Kennel Club, 51 Madison Ave., New York, New York 10010. Your veterinarian or your local dog club can help you with time and place information.

AKC Obedience Trials are divided into three levels of competence: novice, open, and utility. Proficiency at each level must be certified by three different judges. For beginning dogs and trainers, there are six novice exercises: heeling on a leash, heeling off a leash, standing for examination, returning to the trainer when called, sitting until released, and a long down until released. Upon certification, the dog is awarded the title Companion Dog (C.D.).

The Open Class, for those dogs that have achieved the C.D., requires heeling off a leash, going down on command off a leash, retrieving a dumbbell on flat ground, dumbbell retrieving over a high jump and a broad jump, a long sit and a long down. Successful dogs are titled Companion Dog Excellent (C.D.X.).

The coveted Utility Dog certification also has six requirements. First, on signal, the dog must stand, stay, drop, sit, and come. Then, in two separate scent discrimination tests the dog must retrieve one particular article from a set of five. Fourth, when faced with a choice of three white cotton gloves, the dog must retrieve only the glove pointed to by the handler. And finally, the dog must on command clear two hurdles, a bar jump and a high jump. Dogs who complete this demanding exercise earn the honor of having the well-deserved Utility Dog (U.D.) title after their names.

# *If Your Dalmatian Gets Sick*

Most dog owners put a palm to the puppy's nose as a first health check. This is not always a reliable guideline. Although a dog's nose is usually cold and wet, a dry nose itself is not necessarily a sign of illness. Watch for other signs. Sometimes a personality and appetite variance will be the first sign of illness. Obvious signs, such as hair loss or intestinal problems, will alert you even earlier.

## Signs of a Sick Puppy

The bottom line is check your puppy often. If it has a dry nose, feels warm, and won't eat, for instance, or acts listless and drinks a lot more water than usual, it may be ill.

Know your dal's normal temperature. The normal body temperature of a dalmatian is around 101°F (38.3°C). Write down the temperature the veterinarian recorded at the first few puppy checkups. This will give you a baseline for future readings at home. If your dog has a fever, look for other symptoms. Your vet will ask questions about your dog's appetite, general appearance, and recent habits.

## Taking Your Dog's Temperature

Shake down a heavy duty rectal thermometer to about the 96-degree Farenheit mark. Lubricate it, and lift the dog's tail. With a twisting motion, insert the thermometer 1 to 2 inches (2.5–5.1 cm), depending on the size of the dog, into the anal canal. Remove, wipe clean, and read. Normally, a dog's temperature is between 100° and 102°F (37.8°–38.9°C). More than two degrees Farenheit above normal is cause for concern.

## Preventive Medicine

You are your dog's best friend. Your dog's second best friend is your veterinarian and your vet's preventive medicine. Vaccines and similar deterrents build up a dog's natural immunity to the bacteria, viruses, and fungi that cause great pain

for our pets and shorten their lives. These warriors must live and work in the dog's body. Annual boosters keep vaccine levels active.

For puppies born to recently vaccinated parents, a possible schedule would be:
- four weeks—canine distemper;
- eight weeks—canine distemper, infectious canine hepatitis, leptospirosis, parainfluenza, parvovirus (DHLPP);
- twelve weeks—DHLPP, started on heartworm preventive; and
- sixteen weeks—DHLPP, rabies.

## Canine Distemper

Canine distemper is a highly contagious disease caused by a virus. It is most common in unvaccinated puppies in their first year of life. The virus is spread both by direct contact and by airborne particles.

At first the symptoms of canine distemper resemble a common cold. Because dogs don't catch cold, however, you should be suspect of any watery discharge from the dog's eyes and nose. Within days the discharge will turn a thick yellow. Fever, loss of appetite, and listlessness are early symptoms. Later the dog may have epileptic-type seizures. Distemper, easier to prevent than to cure, is the leading cause of infectious deaths in dogs.

The first distemper vaccine should be given shortly after weaning. The breeder usually accepts this responsibility. Consequently, most puppies have their first shots before they go out into the world.

## Viral Hepatitis

Infectious canine hepatitis is a highly contagious disease that can spread to other dogs. Although a dog can have a mild case of hepatitis, the disease also can be deadly and quick acting. It is much more severe when the bacterium *Bordetella* is involved.

Untreated, the disease affects the liver, kidneys, and lining of the blood vessels. In fatal form, the dog suddenly becomes ill, develops bloody diarrhea, collapses, and dies. Puppies show sudden pain and may die before any treatment can be given. There is an effective hepatitis vaccine.

## Leptospirosis

The leptospiral bacteria, found in the urine of an infected animal, for instance, can penetrate unbroken skin. Dogs get leptospirosis from drinking, swimming, or wading in infected water, or from eating infected food. The disease is not contagious to humans as such, but it is caused by an infectious agent, called a spirochete, that can be transmitted to humans and cause disease. The advanced stages of leptospirosis in dogs result in kidney failure. Due to an annual leptospirosis vaccination and boosters, and ever-increasing standards in sanitation practices, this disease no longer is common.

## Rabies

Rabies affects all warm-blooded animals, including man. The saliva of an infected wild animal, such as a fox, skunk, or bat, carries the virus and makes the transfer through a bite. Rabies is fatal to dogs.

The rabies virus inflames the dog's brain. A rabid dog probably will undergo a personality change. The dog may act paralyzed. It may cower or try to hide. It may also turn violent, run, and foam at the mouth.

In some cases, the dog's saliva can be infectious a week before any symptoms appear. Unless you can safely shut the animal up without endangering yourself, don't approach a dog that is acting ugly. Call the authorities. Do not kill the animal. Laboratory tests on a dead animal can be misleading.

A series of treatments has been developed for humans. There is no effective treatment for dogs.

## Canine Parvoviral Disease

Parvoviral disease is highly contagious. Observed in the United States only since 1978, the disease is transmitted from one dog to another through urine and feces. Puppies under five months old have a high mortality to parvovirus.

Two forms of the disease have been noted. In one, symptoms include depression, loss of appetite, vomiting, extreme pain, profuse bloody diarrhea, and high fever. The second form affects the dog's heart muscles. A puppy will stop nursing, cry out, and gasp for breath. Death follows soon after. You can vaccinate your dog against parvovirus.

## Canine Coronaviral Gastroenteritis

Coronaviral gastroenteritis is another relatively new disease that gained prominence in 1978. Nearly indistinguishable from parvoviral disease, and less common, its symptoms can be less severe. The symptoms of coronavirus come on suddenly. A dog that seems well one morning can be vomiting that evening. A general deterioration follows the onset of a persistent diarrhea. Most dogs recover in four to five days. Dogs can be vaccinated against coronavirus.

## Kennel Cough

Infectious tracheobronchitis is a highly contagious disease that spreads rapidly through a group of dogs. The disease lasts several weeks. Even though treated, the dog can be left with chronic bronchitis. Several viruses have been implicated. The parainfluenza vaccine (CPI) protects against one of the viruses. The other, the adenovirus (CAV-2) vaccine, offers double protection both from kennel cough and hepatitis. The presence of the *Bordetella bronchosepticum* bacterium can aggravate either symptom.

## Heartworms

The heartworm larvae are carried by mosquitoes. The larvae from an infective mosquito burrow into the dog. The larvae mature into worms that make their way into the dog's heart and lungs. There the adult worms live and reproduce for about five years, reaching lengths of 4 to 12 inches (10–30 cm). They entwine around and interfere with the dog's heart valves. In untreated dogs, the disease may develop into serious and even fatal complications involving the heart, liver, and kidney.

The dog with heartworms doesn't show any symptoms until very late in the disease. At that time, the number one symptom of heartworm infestation is a soft, dry cough. A second indication is the dog's intolerance for exercise. It can't run as fast or as far as it used to.

The tragedy of heartworm disease is that it can be prevented. Several preparations are on the market. A daily medication kills the larvae before they mature. It does nothing for adult worms and so must be given faithfully during mosquito season to catch the larvae.

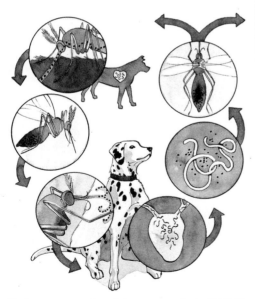

The heartworm requires six to seven months to complete its cycle. Infection begins when an infective mosquito deposits larvae on the dog's skin. The worms burrow into the dog, make their way to a vein, and move to the heart.

The newest heartworm preventive, a monthly tablet, will not only protect against heartworms, but also will protect the dog against another parasite, the common hookworm.

In some parts of the country, the preventive dose is given only during the summer months. In other parts, year-round prevention is the rule. On one occasion, our Louisiana veterinarian who believed in year-round protection checked out a new puppy and pronounced it healthy. Then he tickled the puppy under the chin and said, "You've got a beautiful puppy here. Let's start him on heartworm medication now."

As he spoke, he leaned back to a shelf behind him and picked up what looked like a small canning jar. A dog's heart lay in an autopsy solution. The jar was filled with what appeared to be waving, shiny threads. "This dog was five years old when she had to be put down," he said. "I know you love your puppy, and you're going to do what's right by it. But I tell some clients right off, 'We live in mosquito country. If you love your dog, keep him on the program for life. If you don't, you won't love him for very long.' " The vet put the jar back on the shelf. I reached for the heartworm pills.

## Coat and Skin Problems

### Itching

Dogs sneeze and itch in reaction to allergens, just like we do. Many dogs, not just dalmatians, are allergic to ragweed, tree pollens, grass, wool, house dust, feathers, and molds.

Some dalmatians itch and scratch from spring to summer. This allergic tendency can be hereditary. Chalk up another good reason to purchase from a breeder who has at least one of the parents on hand. Ask to see the dog. Ask questions about skin problems.

If your dal does itch and scratch excessively, ask your veterinarian about trying one of the new anti-inflammatory agents. Omega 3 and omega 6 are two fatty acids that have been proven to reduce itching by as much as 20 percent. They have few side effects. You will find both on the market as diet additives, in ointments, and in flea collars. See your vet.

## Mange

There are two types of mange: demodectic (red mange) and sarcoptic. Both are caused by mites. Both cause loss of hair. Dogs with sarcoptic mange itch and scratch excessively. Demodectic mange does not itch.

Demodectic mange is caused by a mite that lives in the pores of the dog's skin. This mite is present in many dogs and causes problems for only a few. Veterinarians suspect that this lack of response is hereditary. Usually it occurs in puppies three to nine months old whose systems lack the proper immune response to the *Demodex canis* mite.

The first symptom of the disease usually is hair loss from the face and front legs. As it progresses, the hair loss becomes generalized over the entire body. Some untreated puppies make spontaneous recoveries when their immune system develops. The forward progress of the disease is aggravated by inappropriate diet and stress that affects the dog's ability to fight the intrusion. Adolescence, a change in habits, a move to a new location, or jealousy (as when another dog moves in) can bring on an attack.

Dogs with sarcoptic mange have a distinctive, musty odor. The dog scratches because the female mites burrow into its skin to lay eggs. The ear tips often are affected. In fact, crusty ear tips are often a first warning.

Treatment includes use of an insecticide dip once a week for three to four weeks.

## Contact Allergies

A dog can be allergic to almost anything. If your dalmatian develops blisters, a rash, or rosy skin, be prepared to answer your veterinarian's questions about recent life-style changes. Insec-ticides, detergents, soaps, flea powders and collars, plastic and rubber food dishes, and outdoor carpet dyes are common culprits. Don't rule out poison ivy and abrasive houseplants.

## Hot Spots

Hot spots are not uncommon in dalmatians. These weeping, painful bare spots on your dog's coat seem to grow before your eyes. Because our spotted dogs have all the spots they can handle already, some breeders have given particular attention to this problem.

## Skin Tumors

Check your dal at least once a month for skin changes. Older dogs, especially, are prone to tumors. A sore that doesn't heal, or a lump where none should be, is cause to visit your veterinarian. In a female, feel around the breasts. In a male, check the perianal area around the base of the tail. As with humans, early detection of tumors is essential.

## Pests

In summer, the flea and tick problem can get out of control. Many home owners resort to chemical sprays and treated collars. Some of these are very effective. Some dogs, however, are allergic to the chemicals. Some are too young; others are too weak.

Green consumerism is a slogan of the nineties. Your dalmatian can take part, too. Some conscientious owners feed their dogs garlic (which most dogs love) or brewer's yeast. Both are thought to contain natural flea repellents.

Some owners drape colorful, herbal collars filled with any of several aromatic powders around their pet's neck. Other owners purchase expensive high-frequency ultrasound collars. Even if you are not already a believer in herbal or electronic flea control, you might like to try one of these alternative methods. Some veterinarians doubt the efficacy of both herb and electronic controls. If you do try one and it works, no one can argue with success.

**Fleas:** The flea is the most common parasite on dogs. Because the flea lives by feeding on blood, a severe infestation can cause anemia.

The secret to flea control is to treat the environment. The flea has no wings and cannot fly, but it can jump long distances. In fact, the flea spends much of its life off of the dog in furniture cracks, cushions, bedding, and carpets.

Mild flea shampoos and insecticide dips remove the pests themselves, but the effect is short lasting. To be effective, treatment must continue for four weeks. It must involve a product with growth regulators, ovacides, that wipe out the egg population as well as kill the adult fleas.

See your veterinarian for a proved insecticidal product. Then consider this inside-the-house program. Every week, for four weeks, vacuum the carpet, the furniture, and the dog's pen. Burn the vacuum bag. Wash the dog's bedding. Sprinkle the house with the recommended insecticide. Treat the yard. In addition, on the first and third weeks of the program, shampoo your dog. The program is arduous but effective.

**Ticks:** Ticks are found in the woods, in the park, in your backyard. Ticks mate, however, on your dog. Look for the feeding female tick on your dog's ears, under its neck, or between its toes. The female sometimes swells to about the size and color of a bean. When you find the female, look for the male tick. Often referred to as a seed tick, the male is small and flat, and nearby.

First, kill the female tick. Dip a cotton applicator in alcohol. Hold it on the tick's body. Then catch the tick as close to your dog's skin as possible and pull steadily. Examine the tick to be sure you have the head. Lift the male tick off with tweezers. Dab the spot with alcohol.

All ticks are capable of transmitting some disease. One, however, the *Ixodes ricinus* tick, has been the subject of much national press. Spirochetes from this tick enter man and cause Lyme disease. Named in 1975 for the Connecticut community that gave it its name, Lyme is now the most frequent tick-borne disease in humans. The disease can be debilitating and even fatal.

The first symptoms are the presence of a round or oval shaped skin rash at the site of the bite. Flu-like symptoms of headache, muscle soreness, fever, and fatigue follow. In severe cases, joint pain, facial paralysis, and heart problems add to the complications.

Recent strides were made in prevention when the U.S. Department of Agriculture granted conditional licensing for a "first generation" vaccine against Lyme, approved on a state-to-state basis. Check with your veterinarian for details.

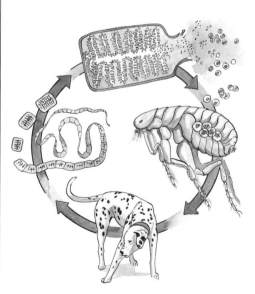

Tapeworms, commonly transmitted by the flea, live in the small intestine. Body segments about 1/4 inch (.6 cm) long are passed in the dog's stool. When dry, the segments resemble uncooked rice.

# *If Your Dalmatian Gets Sick*

## Worms

Most puppies are born with worms. Deworming should be done on each litter at two to three weeks of age, and again at five to six weeks. Many adult dogs are subject to worms; the most common types are the tapeworm and roundworm. Because adult roundworms are very hardy and can live for months or years in soil, some breeders routinely deworm their adult dogs once a year.

An interesting side effect of daily heartworm medication is that it offers some protection against roundworms. One monthly preventive specifically kills adult hookworms.

## Eyes, Ears, Mouth, and Feet Disorders

A dalmatian's eyes should be bright and responsive. They rarely tear. They require no special attention.

A dalmatian's ears seldom have to be cleaned. Some wax, in fact, is beneficial. If your dog obviously has foreign material in its ear, you may have to clean it out. Dip a clean piece of cloth in mineral oil. Wrap the cloth around the tip of your

A dal's eyes should be round, bright, and clear. In black-spotted puppies, darker is better. In liver-brown dogs, the eyes should be golden, light brown, or amber colored.

Dalmatians and other drop-eared breeds are subject to earflap hematoma caused by violent head shaking or scratching. Consequently, any sudden earflap swelling should be looked at and treated as soon as possible.

finger and wipe around the inside of the ear flap. Don't go any further.

If your dog shakes its head, scratches at its ears, or if you notice a foul odor or discharge, contact your veterinarian.

Healthy gums are firm and pink. A dalmatian's teeth should overlap in a scissor bite, like yours. A puppy will shed its baby teeth at four to five months of age. Sometimes if this process is delayed or the teeth get pulled early, the bite can be affected. It's wise to check a puppy's bite once a month until it is at least six months old. A faulty bite caught early can be corrected.

Many owners brush their dog's teeth with a child's toothbrush dipped in a 3 percent hydrogen peroxide solution. This removes lodged particles but does nothing for tartar. Tartar buildup is not normal. If you find tartar on your dal's teeth, tell your veterinarian.

A dalmatian walks up on its toes, like a cat. The breed has a tendency to go flat-footed if its nails are too long. Yard dalmatians seldom have this trouble. If yours is a house dalmatian, though, it is possible that you'll have to clip the dog's nails every month

# *If Your Dalmatian Gets Sick*

Dogs usually don't have cavities, but they do develop tartar. A daily dog bisquit, a large knuckle bone once a week, and an occasional brushing will do much to prevent problems later on.

Avoid cutting into the pink part, the "quick," of the nail. Should it bleed, apply pressure with a cotton ball, or use a styptic (such as used for shaving).

or so. Besides direct observation, the best way to tell when it's time to cut is to listen to your dalmatian when it walks on a wooden floor. If you hear a click, cut.

## Diarrhea, Vomiting, Constipation

An occasional soft stool isn't a cause for worry. A dog will get diarrhea as a result of indiscreet eating. Garbage, milk, rich food, a change in diet, and toxic plants often have a laxative effect.

If your dog has mild diarrhea, try cutting back on its food. Offer only dry kibble. Continued diarrhea is serious. If the symptoms have not disappeared by the next day, take your dog to the veterinarian.

Like diarrhea, the normal rule is that we don't worry about casual vomiting. A rule of thumb: If your dog throws up once or twice and then acts normal, it probably is okay. If vomiting persists, however, call your veterinarian.

Most healthy dogs have one or two stools a day. To qualify as constipation, a dog should have difficulty passing a stool. It could show signs of pain. Sometimes an older male has difficulty because an enlarged prostate bulges into the anal canal. This is a situation for your veterinarian.

If small, hard stools are normal for your dog and not painful, you should have no worry. Try switching to another kibble. Or add a little bran cereal, celery, or whole wheat bread to your dog's diet.

## How To Give Medicine

If you have to give your pet a pill, you might take advantage of a dog's tendency to bolt its food. Coat the pill with peanut butter or wrap it in cheese. Offer one lump of plain peanut butter, for instance, and the coated capsule the next time. The dog probably will swallow it happily.

Otherwise, place the pill in the middle and well to the back of your dal's mouth. Hold its jaws together with one hand and gently stroke its throat with the other. You should see a swallow. Praise. Be observant because dalmatians are wonderfully adept at concealing the pill and spitting it back at you later.

# *If Your Dalmatian Gets Sick*

The correct way to give a pill: Place the pill in the middle and well to the back of your dal's mouth.

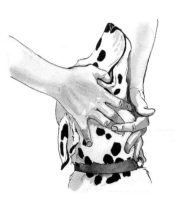

Close the dog's mouth and hold it shut while stroking the dog's throat. If the dog swallows, or licks its nose, probably it swallowed the pill.

Liquid medicine is best poured into a lip pocket. Ask someone to help you the first few times until you and the dog get the hang of it. Let the assistant hold the bottle and dropper or spoon. Calm your dog. Make it sit. Tilt its head back.

Using your fingers, pull out the dog's lower lip at the corner where the upper and lower lips join. Have your assistant pour medicine into this nice, convenient pouch. The medicine should dribble between the teeth and down the throat. Praise.

## Weighing Your Dalmatian

Because accurate dosage depends on the dog's weight, you often will have to know how much your dog weighs. It is not easy to get your dalmatian on a scale.

A simple solution is to step on the scale alone. Weigh yourself. Read the scale and write down the numbers. Bend over and pick up your dal. Weigh both of you. Read the scale. The difference in the two figures is the dog's weight.

## Emergencies

Emergencies are sudden illnesses or traumas that require immediate care. You should be familiar with some animal aid techniques to help you stabilize your pet until a vet can be called.

### Shock

A dog will go into shock just like people do. Any severe trauma, such as broken bones, internal injury, or copious bleeding, can send a dog into shock. When the dog's circulation slows, its vital organs don't get enough oxygen. The body temperature lowers, the dog shivers and is weak. Its legs and feet chill. Prolonged shock can cause death.

Get help. While waiting, speak soothingly to the dog. Cover it. If you have to move the dog (out of the road, for instance), be careful. An injured dog given further pain will snap and bite.

An injured dog can bite, though unintentionally. In an emergency, a makeshift muzzle can be made from a torn strip of cloth or a necktie.

## Snakebites

Inquisitive dalmatians often will bat at a snake or a lizard. Even a nonpoisonous snakebite can be painful. Bites most often occur on the nose, tongue, or face. A bite on the head can swell alarmingly. In fact, you should suspect a snakebite if the swelling is obvious and grows as you watch it. Get the dog to the veterinarian immediately. Your vet probably has on hand the antivenin for the poisonous snakes in your area. For the best chance of recovery, the antivenin should be given within two hours.

## Stinging Insects

We rarely observe spider, bee, or wasp stings. Our first indication of a sting is a fast and localized swelling, often on an ear flap. A spider bite results in an intense itching, which doesn't subside for 8 to 12 hours. A bee will leave a stinger behind, which you must pull out with tweezers or your fingernails. In some instances, however, the actual location of the bite may never be determined.

After any insect sting, watch your dog carefully. Provided that the dog is not having a severe reaction, apply a paste of baking soda and calamine lotion. Your pet probably would appreciate an ice pack. Within two hours, if the swelling has not subsided, or your dog is still in obvious pain, contact your veterinarian.

## Poisoning

The symptoms of poisoning are pain, panting, shivering, convulsions, and coma. If your dog hasn't been out of the yard, look to your own garden. Could it have chewed plants that have been sprayed recently? Could it have followed you around the yard and gulped slug bait? Does your car engine leak? That sweet-tasting antifreeze on the driveway is poisonous. If you suspect poisoning, get your pet to the veterinarian immediately.

## Bleeding

The best treatment for bleeding is to apply pressure and a tourniquet enroute to a veterinarian. A tourniquet closes the blood vessels between the injury and the heart. If you will reach the veterinarian within 30 minutes you probably can leave the tourniquet on. Otherwise, loosen the tourniquet for two to three minutes every 30 minutes.

## Fractures

A dog that has been hit by a car can have massive internal injuries. A dog that tangles with a bicycle or one that falls off a porch might be lucky enough to sustain only a fracture. A broken leg is the most common fracture. Keep in mind that the leg will have to be set professionally. Your problem is to get the dog to a veterinarian with as little trauma as possible.

First, try to keep the dog calm. A snapped bone grinding against muscle can cause extensive damage. Try not to move the dog until you can get a splint on the leg.

Straighten the leg as much as you can. Use whatever is on hand—a yardstick, broom handle, magazine, or heavy cardboard tube—to immobilize the limb. Wrap the splint with gauze, torn strips of cotton, anything handy. Call your veterinarian immediately.

# *Breeding Your Dalmatian*

## Puppy Love

Taking care of a litter has been called true puppy love. After whelping, you will be on duty night and day for seven to eight weeks.

It is true that for the first three weeks your primary responsibility will be to the dam. Up to that time, if she is fed and exercised properly, a healthy mama dalmatian will tend to her brood with minimal help from you. Your job will be to see to it that Mama has the right environment in which to do her job. She will keep her litter of eight to ten puppies warm, full, contented, and sanitary. After three weeks, though, the ball will be in your court.

From that day on, each puppy will demand your attention three or four times a day. This attention can take the form of supplemental feeding, nursing care, grooming, cleaning, nail clipping, deworming, or socializing.

## Why Breed?

Why do we do it? Look into your own reasons for breeding. Don't breed your female dalmatian if you don't have time to spend with the litter. From weeks three to seven you must set aside an hour or two, sometimes four times a day, to help.

Don't breed because dalmatian puppies are so cute. A backyard full of eight-week-old dalmatian puppies is more mischief than cute.

Don't breed because you feel having a litter would be interesting for the children. Children have a way of losing interest.

Don't breed to make money. You won't.

Breed your dalmatian only if you sincerely believe that the litter will produce beautiful pups sent to loving homes. Breed only because you have a sincere commitment to quality. If you have the commitment, the dalmatian fancy will welcome you.

That said, let's see how best to approach this new challenge.

## Your Responsibilities as a Breeder

If you plan to breed your dalmatian, one of your first responsibilities is to assure yourself that your dog, stud or bitch, is healthy. Consult your veterinarian.

For the most part, this chapter deals with owners of females who will bear the litter at home. The first two categories though are applicable to both stud and bitch.

Before you breed, ask yourself, is your dalmatian a quality dog that could be a show winner? Is its conformation and temperament all you could ask for? Do neighbors and friends and strangers comment on how beautiful your dog is? Do they ask for puppies?

Is your dalmatian free of inherited defects, deafness, mange? Has it been tested for canine brucellosis, an infectious bacterial disease spread in the breeding process?

For the owners of the dam, do you have a list of people who want puppies? Many breeders won't consider a litter until a substantial list of acceptable homes is waiting for the puppies.

Do you have the time to keep accurate records of matings, litters, and pedigrees? Are you ready to read and learn as much as you can on whelping, genetics, and temperament training?

Is there space in your home or your backyard for a nursery?

Are you willing to spend over an hour with the mama dog and puppies, four times a day for seven or eight weeks? Such miscellaneous necessities as cleaning out the whelping box or pen, clipping nails, deworming, and feeding training are satisfyingly challenging but time-consuming chores.

Are you ready to assume the additional expense incurred by veterinarian visits, food, and vaccinations? Have you figured in the cost of advertising the litter?

Are you ready to stand by your puppies and take them back if things don't work out? Will you refund money if something is unexpectedly wrong? Do you plan to assess the prospective buyers for temperament matches and housing accommodations? Will you reject buyers who don't have the proper understanding of what is involved in raising a dalmatian?

Have you thought about what you will do if the litter doesn't sell by nine or ten weeks?

## Choosing a Mate

Now that you have made the decision to breed your dalmatian, to which line will you breed—an immediate relative, the dalmatian down the street, or a stud offered in a national magazine?

The decision will depend on the qualities of your line that you would like reinforced or subjugated. Breeding for quality is a complicated issue. Every major kennel studies its breeding stock. Take a good look at your dalmatian. With a copy of the standard before you, assess the dog's strong points and its weaknesses. Think back to the day you made your own selection. Was it that intelligent expression that captured your heart? Or was it those compact, well-arched feet?

Try to pay a visit to some of your dalmatian's littermates. Do those pretty feet run in the litter? Or is yours the only one that's outstanding and the rest are just passable? Maybe you would like to strengthen that feature. You can guess the answer. Among a long list of other things, you will be sure you also "breed to a pretty foot."

The above is a too-simplified version of breeding. Despite generations of careful selection, no line, of course, breeds consistently perfect dogs. Anyhow, the perfect dalmatian probably doesn't exist. Many dalmatians, however, have come very close. And that's what good breeding is all about.

**Outcrossing, Inbreeding, Linebreeding:** The three major breeding methods are defined by the degree of common ancestry of the two dogs involved.

A breed is said to be *outcrossed* when the two dogs share no common ancestors over the last five or six generations.

A line is *inbred* if the mating is of two immediate relatives. A brother to sister, son to mother, for example, is inbreeding.

*Linebreeding* is breeding to any relative beyond the immediate (grandparents, uncles, and so on). Linebreeding usually is considered to be the safest and surest path to take when breeding an already quality line.

## Practicalities

The owner of the female almost always travels to the male. In recent years, the ease of artificial insemination has given breeders additional options. Frozen sperm from stud dogs long past their prime can be utilized.

Whatever the technique used, a fee traditionally is charged for the service. This fee can be in the form of a standard payment, or what is called a "pick of the litter" payment. Sometimes the two are combined.

Usually the stud fee is paid at the time of mating. If the female does not conceive, the male's owner may offer a return service but is not obligated to do so. When agreeing to a "pick of the litter" stud fee, it is wise to agree ahead of time on the puppy's age at pick.

Most vets recommend a vaccination booster for the female before breeding to increase antibodies in the litter. At that time, have her tested for parasites and dewormed if necessary. Both dogs should be certified free of brucellosis and other canine diseases.

The female should not be bred until the second heat. She then can be bred every other heat after that date until she is six or seven years old. The

If you decide to show your dal, attend several events, ▶ watch the dogs and handlers, and make arrangements for further instruction.

# Breeding Your Dalmatian

male should be at least one year old, and not greater than seven, before breeding.

**When Is Your Female Ready?:** The most common cause of an unsuccessful mating is to attempt breeding during the wrong part of the estrus cycle. A mature dalmatian female usually comes into heat and therefore can conceive, every six to eight months. Generally, this heat lasts 21 days, which can be divided into three periods.

During the first period, the vulva swells and male dogs are attracted to her. For six to nine days, she usually will growl or snap or sit when the males approach. If you don't plan to breed your female, now is the time to confine her. Be very sure that she can't dig her way out and that male dogs can't jump the fence or dig under it.

If your dalmatian is a house dog, put her on a leash for walks. Try to get some distance away from the house, to a public park, if possible, before letting her eliminate. Distance will help to confuse suitors.

Actual estrus, often called standing heat, occurs for the next six to twelve days. During this time, the female will accept the male. Usually, she will "flag" her tail, that is, hold it aside, and stand quietly. This period is the best time for conception. Many breeders breed at least twice, on the second and fourth day, or the third and fifth day, of standing heat.

The third part of the actual estrus cycle concludes with a gradual waning of interest of all parties and a subsequent hardening of the vulva.

**Spaying and Neutering:** Females do not need to have a litter to be complete. Spaying is a surgical procedure that will prevent her from having puppies. Spaying is best done after a female is six months of age and before her first heat.

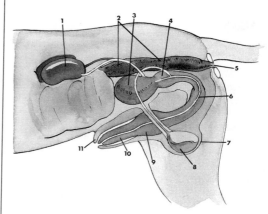

The reproductive organs of the male dalmatian:
1. kidneys
2. rectum
3. bladder
4. prostate
5. anus
6. urethra
7. scrotum
8. testes
9. bulb
10. penis
11. sheath

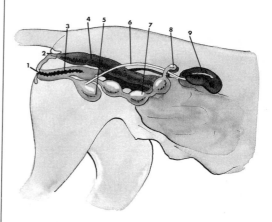

The reproductive organs of the female dalmatian:
1. vulva
2. anus
3. vagina
4. rectum
5. bladder
6. ureter
7. developing embryo
8. ovary
9. kidney

◀ Some dals are natural show dogs. Paired with an owner-handler who enjoys the ring, they trot easily through the required routines.

# *Breeding Your Dalmatian*

Neutering is an operation on male dogs in which both testicles are removed. Because the operation often affects the dog's secondary sex characteristics, it is best to wait until the dog is grown. Neutering often cures males from wandering.

**The First Mating:** Neither animal should be fed for several hours before mating. One handler comfortable with each dog should be present. If the dogs do not know each other, both dogs should be on a leash. The procedure is easier all around if at least one of the dogs is experienced, but nature usually steps in and the act takes place without help.

If the female is ready, the male will mount her from the rear holding her loins with his forelegs while thrusting.

**The Tie:** The tie is unique to canines. A bulb (a knot at the base of the penis) swells and the female's vaginal muscles contract behind it. The two are thus tied together anywhere from 10 to 45 minutes. The male usually will instinctively throw one hind leg over the female's back and turn so that the two are standing back to back. Here is where a handler can help. If the dogs do not turn back-to-back, lift one of the male's hind legs and turn him.

Because the tie is a natural and necessary part of the mating, never try to separate the dogs. They may be uncomfortable, but are not in danger. The canine penis, on the other hand, contains a bone that could break if enough force is applied.

Remember the mating date. It will be necessary to provide the date when you apply for litter registration.

## Care and Feeding During Pregnancy

The average length of gestation is nine weeks (63 days). During this waiting period, continue to exercise your female every day. She will be healthier and better able to withstand the drain of whelping and nursing.

Feed her a normal maintenance diet until the fourth or fifth week of pregnancy. By four weeks her protein requirements will have increased, so you might want to switch to a puppy formula kibble that is higher in protein. The growing puppies might be pushing on her stomach. If she doesn't finish her meal as usual, maybe she's uncomfortable. Her puppies might be crowding her stomach and she might not have room for a large meal. If you normally feed once a day, try feeding the same amount twice a day.

During weeks six to nine, when she's providing nourishment for growing puppies, increase her ration one-half, dividing it into three smaller meals a day. Watch her weight. Don't let her get fat.

At least two weeks before you expect to need it, prepare a place for the whelping. A clean, dry, draft-free box is best. If your dal is a house dog, she will prefer to be near you at this time, so choose the site with care.

## The Whelping Box

The traditional dalmatian whelping box is about 4 by 5 feet (1.2 x 1.5 m). Its sides are at least 12 inches (30 cm) high. It is constructed with a 3-inch (7.6 cm) ledge around the inside of the box. This ledge offers extra protection, preventing the dam from rolling on the puppies and accidentally crushing or smothering them.

The whelping box should be located in a quiet, out-of-the-way spot. Select a location that is clean, dry, draft-free, and warm.

Layer several sheets of clean newspaper on the bottom of the box. On top of the newspapers place heavy towels, mattress pads, indoor-outdoor carpeting, or any disposable or washable material.

Introduce your female to the box at least two weeks before you expect to need it. If she will, insist that she sleep in the box.

## Whelping Accessories

Once the mother's bed has been outfitted, turn your attention to a support box of your own. Line a small cardboard box with newspaper. Cover the paper with a towel. Add a hot water bottle or a heating pad, a postal scale that will register up to two pounds, a notebook and pencil, packages of colored rickrack, a flashlight, a bulb syringe, dental floss, scissors, and iodine. On top of the support box, place a stack of newspapers and a stack of clean towels. Store the box in a convenient place.

## Helping in Labor

The first stage of labor begins with rapid panting and straining. The dalmatian female is an easy whelper and a good mother. She rarely needs help, but she would appreciate your presence.

When labor begins, get your support box down. Empty it of everything except the layer of paper on the bottom and the towel on top. Warm the box. Fill the hot water bottle or turn on the heating pad. Settle down nearby with a book or TV show. Don't hover.

When a puppy is born, it is encased in a fetal membrane. Usually, the mother tears open the fetal sack and licks the puppy to stimulate its breathing. It is very important that this membrane be removed within 30 seconds. If the mother doesn't do it, you will have to. Starting at the puppy's mouth, remove the membranes. Use your bulb syringe to remove any secretions from the puppy's mouth. Briskly rub the puppy with a soft towel to stimulate it. Present the puppy to the mother. Fill the hot water bottle.

In a few minutes, the mother will roll the puppy around and sever the umbilical cord by shredding it with her teeth. Leave her alone even if she seems rough. She probably will do a good job.

The placenta usually will follow the puppy in a few moments. The mother instinctively will eat this afterbirth. Leave her alone. Eating the placenta does no harm and may help her milk production.

The remaining puppies should appear at regular intervals, usually from 15 minutes to an hour or more apart. It's your turn again. When the second puppy is about to appear, place the first puppy in that warm box you fixed up earlier. Do the same for each succeeding puppy.

In between births, put the puppies to the mama's nipples. Their sucking action helps draw down the colostrum, which is very important to their health. Use this time to check the puppies to be sure the cords are not bleeding. Weigh and identify the puppies.

Use your own judgment about leaving the room. If everything is going smoothly, the mother will rest between births. Even so, some new mamas don't want you out of their sight. If you leave, your dal will get out of the box to follow you, presenting a new puppy at your feet if necessary. If you can leave, be sure to check on her every 20 minutes or so.

## When To Get Professional Help

Instinctively, the mother dog knows what is needed. It is best not to interfere. But there are some situations where your help could make all the difference. After all, that's why you're with her. That's why you have a good relationship with your veterinarian. Your veterinarian would prefer to be called on a false alarm than to lose the puppies and perhaps the mother.

Call your veterinarian:
- if the mama dog is straining and in hard and serious labor for two hours without delivering a puppy;

- if a large puppy gets stuck in the vaginal opening (you'll know, because the presenting part appears and disappears with each contraction);
- if she passes dark green or bloody fluid before the birth of the first puppy (Green or bloody fluid is not abnormal after the first puppy.); or
- if labor stops and there are continued signs of restlessness and anxiety.

## The Care of Puppies

After all the puppies have been delivered, begin the task of cleaning up. The mother will be tired. Check each puppy for malformations. Check the cord again. Sometimes the mother shreds the cord too close to the puppy's navel. If a stump is bleeding, get the dental floss from your support box. Make a loop around the stump and tie it firmly in place with a square knot.

Weigh the puppies again at 12 hours and at 24 hours. The majority of puppies, at 24 hours, will have gained weight. If any puppy shows a significant weight loss (more than 10 percent) call your veterinarian for instructions.

Individual identification of newborn dalmatians is difficult. Dalmatian puppies are born pure white. (See the color photograph of newly born dalmatian puppies on page 9.)

True spots do not appear until the puppies are ten days to two weeks old. About all you can tell for sure is some are male and some are female. Consequently, record keeping in a large litter can be a challenge.

Be creative. Some breeders rely on colored baby rickrack, slipping a different color around each puppy's neck. (That's not as many colors as you might think at first glance, because there can be a male red and a female red.) The dam does not appear to mind the rickrack. If you do use rickrack, remember to check the fit daily. If the mother does object to the rickrack, try a dot of nail polish on a tiny toenail. With 20 nails to choose from on each puppy, you ought to come up with a workable code.

## Patched Puppies

Dalmatian puppies are born pure white. If a puppy is born with an area of solid color, that color is usually a "patch" and not a "spot." Patches are genetically undesirable.

What's the problem? In order to understand the breeder's dismay over a patch, let's look at the overall dalmatian standard. The breed's unique coloration is one of its distinctions. The dal's spots are not square nor oblong, but round. They are not large nor irregular, but relatively small and unmistakable "spots." The standard says, "The spots should not intermingle, but be as round and well defined as possible, the more distinct the better. In size they should be from that of a dime to a half-dollar. Patches...constitute a disqualification."

Patches can occur anywhere on the body, but most often are found on the ears and head. The typical patch is present at birth. It is black or liver colored with no visible white hairs. The texture of the hair on a patch may be somewhat softer than the rest of the hairs.

No responsible breeder will sell a patched puppy. Because patching is probably hereditary, breeders sometimes have puppies that are born with patches put to sleep. At the least, such puppies are sold with specific spaying or neutering prohibitions.

## New Puppies

Chilling is the greatest danger to newborn puppies. A puppy is born the same temperature as its mother. Its temperature drops immediately after birth. Keep the floor temperature of the whelping box at 85°F (30°C) for at least the first week. Reduce the temperature five degrees each week for three weeks, then set it permanently at 70°F (21°C). Remember to leave some space away from the heat for the dam. She may need a cooler spot to rest in.

Ten percent of the puppies whelped do not survive the first two weeks of life. Seventy-five percent of these die during the first four days. A variety of factors have been identified. The puppy may have developed a bacterial infection. Some puppies, that have no obvious problems and apparently are healthy at birth, won't eat and lose strength rapidly. These puppies are classic examples of what is called fading puppy syndrome.

## Are Your Puppies Healthy?

At birth, a puppy cannot hear or see. Generally, by ten days, a puppy's eyes open, and, though wobbly, it can stand. By two weeks, the puppy can hear. At three weeks, still wobbly, it can walk.

- Expect your puppies from birth to three weeks, to sleep 90 percent and eat 10 percent of the time. If a puppy cries for more than ten minutes before falling asleep, call your veterinarian.
- A newborn puppy sleeps with its head curled under its chest. By the third day, a healthy puppy will stretch out. If one of your new litter is still in a curled position at three days, call your veterinarian.
- A healthy puppy, when removed from the dam, will try to crawl back to her. Weak puppies cannot maintain a high enough temperature to survive. They are limp and cold. They are not interested in nursing. They fall asleep away from their littermates. The mother will make little or no effort to coax a chilled or ill puppy back to her. Call your veterinarian.

## Saving a Weak Puppy

Some breeders refuse to let nature take its course. If you must intervene personally, remember that the puppy's body temperature must be brought up as quickly as possible. Don't waste any time. Place the newborn next to your own skin, letting your body heat transfer to the puppy while setting up an incubator.

Put a heating pad on the bottom of a cardboard box. Cover the pad with a lightweight cloth or diaper. Adjust a high heat overhead light. Put a thermometer in the bottom of the box. Adjust the temperature so that the reading is 85° to 90°F (30° – 32°C). Warming can take two to three hours. The

puppy should stay in the incubator until it can maintain its own body termperature, about 94°F (34°C).

As soon as possible, put the puppy back with the litter to nurse. Watch it carefully. If it is too weak, if its body temperature drops again, or if the dam rejects it, consider hand feeding.

Puppies may be fed by spoon, eye dropper, preemie nursing bottle, or stomach tube. Your veterinarian can make a recommendation.

## Growth Rate in Puppies

After the 24 hours checkup, record each puppy's weight weekly. Healthy puppies will double their birth weight in eight to ten days. Weight gain should be steady. Notice and make a record of each puppy's appetite, stool quality, and temperament.

## Feeding Puppies

At four weeks, offer the puppies two meals each day of a puppy kibble softened in a bitch's milk replacer and warm water. (Cow's milk is not suitable for rearing puppies.) When the puppies are eating well, offer four meals and gradually reduce the milk. Let the dam nurse them as long as she will at night. Gradually substitute canned dog food or cottage cheese for some of the milk.

By seven weeks, when the puppy is ready for a new home, it should be eating 90 percent dry kibble with 10 percent canned meat or cottage cheese.

## Acquiring Your Litter's Registration Papers

Within a week of delivery, as soon as you are sure the puppies have made it through that treacherous first week, apply to the AKC for litter registration.

Upon receipt of your application and the appropriate fee (which at the time of writing was $15), the AKC will send you a set of partially prepared registration application blue forms—one for each puppy in the litter. One completed application is to be given to each new owner.

## Full or Limited Registration?

In January 1990, the AKC, in a move intended to strengthen the breeds, allowed breeders to identify their litters as to quality. Before registering today's litter, the litter owner must make a decision. Are these puppies, though purebred, top specimens of their line? Are they suitable for show or breeding? If these are considered top of the line dogs, the litter is registered as usual.

Those litters, although purebred, that are destined to be sold as family pets, are issued limited registration. Limited registration applies to the entire litter. It prevents their offspring, if any, from being registered. No puppy with limited registration can be shown. It does not, however, prohibit the dog from entering (and winning) obedience trials or tracking and hunting tests.

There is a procedure for revoking limited registration, but usually this limitation remains with the dog forever.

## Choosing a Home for Your Puppies

After all the work and worry, you are not about to send your little charges off to the wild blue outdoors without a good idea of what kind of future life they can expect. Although two-page questionnaires are not unheard of, most breeders stick to simple queries:

- Is this your first dog? If not, what happened to the others?
- Do you have a fenced-in yard? If not, what plans do you have for exercise?
- Do you have children? What ages are they?
- Is there a veterinarian nearby?

Members of the Dalmatian Club of America pledge not to consign their puppies to pet stores or wholesalers. They will not supply dogs for raffles or giveaways. Most ask that if for some reason one anticipates a move, or unexpected expenses, the puppy be returned to them.

## Traveling Papers

Send your puppies to their new homes with a carefully thought-out puppy kit. A good kit includes:

- the completed AKC registration application (the "blue" slip);
- the puppy's medical record;
- a three-generation pedigree;
- an instruction sheet including such information as bringing the puppy home, housebreaking, diet, grooming, and training. A brief explanation of hereditary problems;
- a small supply of the puppy's food and a gallon jug of its water;
- literature regarding crate training, obedience classes, breed club information, and pet supply company catalogs; and
- photos of the puppy's parents and any pictures of baby days.

These dals had a head start. They inherited good dispositions and sturdy genes from both parents. Their new owners were selected with care. They should lead a long and healthy life.

# *Characteristics of the Breed*

## An Overview

The dalmatian will not be mistaken for any other breed. On the street, strangers will stop to admire the alert, friendly dog at your side. In the show ring, handlers will bless the dalmatian's obvious enthusiasm for pageantry. Judges will comment on the dal's well-defined head and its wagging saber tail. But no one — casual passerby, owner, or show judge — fails to notice the dalmatian's spots. The breed's joyful, unique coloration, along with its history of mannerly behavior, seems to have endowed the dalmatian with an acceptance rare in dogdom. Even people who have no interest in dogs will instantly recognize your pet as a dalmatian and, more likely than not, will be won over by its alert and cheerful demeanor.

The official standard is a description of the ideal dalmatian. It outlines in precise language the characteristics of a championship dal. Breeders study the conformation of their own dogs with the standard in mind. The standard is the breeder's guide.

## The Official Dalmatian Standard

### General Appearance

The dalmatian is a distinctively spotted dog; poised and alert; strong, muscular and active; free of shyness; intelligent in expression; symmetrical in outline; and without exaggeration or coarseness. The dalmatian is capable of great endurance, combined with a fair amount of speed.

Deviations from the described ideal should be personalized in direct proportion to the degree of the deviation.

### Size, Proportion, Substance

Desirable height at the withers is between 19 and 23 inches (48–58 cm). Undersize or oversize is a fault. Any dog or bitch over 24 inches (61 cm) at the withers is disqualified.

The overall length of the body from the forechest to the buttocks is approximately equal to the height at the withers.

The dalmatian has good substance and is strong and sturdy in bone, but never coarse.

### Head

The head is in balance with the overall dog. It is of fair length and is free of loose skin. The dalmatian's **expression** is alert and intelligent, indicating a stable and outgoing temperament.

The **eyes** are set moderately well apart, are medium sized and somewhat rounded in appearance, and are set well into the skull. Eye color is brown or blue, or any combination thereof; the darker the better and usually darker in black-spotted than in liver-spotted dogs.

Abnormal position of the eyelids or eyelashes (ectropion, entropion, trichiasis) is a major fault.

Incomplete pigmentation of the eye rims is a major fault.

The **ears** are of moderate size, proportionately wide at the base and gradually tapering to a rounded tip. They are set rather high, and are carried close to the head, and are thin and fine in texture. When the dalmatian is alert, the top of the ear is level with the top of the skull and the tip of the ear reaches to the bottom line of the cheek.

The top of the skull is flat with a slight vertical furrow and is approximately as wide as it is long. The **stop** is moderately well defined. The cheeks blend smoothly into a powerful **muzzle**, the top of which is level and parallel to the top of the skull. The muzzle and the top of the skull are about equal in length.

The **nose** is completely pigmented on the leather, black in black-spotted dogs and brown in liver-spotted dogs. Incomplete nose pigmentation is a major fault.

The **lips** are clean and close fitting. The teeth meet in a **scissors bite**. Overshot or undershot bites are disqualifications.

### Neck, Topline, Body

The **neck** is nicely arched, fairly long, free

from throatiness, and blends smoothly into the shoulders.

The **topline** is smooth.

The **chest** is deep, capacious and of moderate width, having good spring of rib without being barrel shaped. The brisket reaches to the elbow. The underline of the rib cage curves gradually into a moderate tuck-up.

The **back** is level and strong. The **loin** is short, muscular and slightly arched. The flanks narrow through the loin. The **croup** is nearly level with the back.

The **tail** is a natural extension of the topline. It is not inserted too low down. It is strong at the insertion and tapers to the tip, which reaches to the hock. It is never docked. The tail is carried with a slight upward curve but should never curl over the back. Ring tails and low-set tails are faults.

## Forequarters

The **shoulders** are smoothly muscled and well laid back. The **upper arm** is approximately equal in length to the shoulder blade and joins it at an angle sufficient to insure that the foot falls under the shoulder. The **elbows** are close to the body. The **legs** are straight, strong and sturdy in bone. There is a slight angle at the **pastern** denoting flexibility.

## Hindquarters

The **hindquarters** are powerful, having smooth, yet well defined muscles. The **stifle** is well bent. The **hocks** are well let down. When the dalmatian is standing, the hind legs, viewed from the rear, are parallel to each other from the point of the hock to the heel of the pad. Cowhocks are a major fault.

## Feet

**Feet** are very important. Both front and rear feet are round and compact with thick, elastic pads and well arched toes. Flat feet are a major fault. Toenails are black and/or white in black-spotted dogs and brown and/or white in liver-spotted dogs. Dewclaws may be removed.

## Coat

The **coat** is short, dense, fine and close fitting. It is neither wooly nor silky. It is sleek, glossy and healthy in appearance.

## Color and Markings

**Color and markings** and their overall appearance are very important points to be evaluated.

The ground color is pure white. In black-spotted dogs the spots are dense black. In liver-spotted dogs the spots are liver brown. Any color markings other than black or liver are disqualified.

**Spots** are round and well-defined, the more distinct the better. They vary from the size of a dime to the size of a half-dollar. They are pleasingly and evenly distributed. The less the spots intermingle the better. Spots are usually smaller on the head, legs and tail than on the body. Ears are preferably spotted.

**Tri-color** (which occurs rarely in this breed) is a disqualification. It consists of tan markings found on the head, neck, chest leg or tail of a black-or-liver-spotted dog. Bronzing of black spots, and fading and/or darkening of liver spots due to environmental conditions or normal processes of coat change are not tri-coloration.

**Patches** are a disqualification. A patch is a solid mass of black or liver hair containing no white hair. It is appreciably larger than a normal size spot. Patches are a dense, brilliant color with sharply defined, smooth edges. Patches are present at birth. Large color masses formed by intermingled or overlapping spots are not patches. Such masses should indicate individual spots by uneven edges and/or white hairs scattered throughout the mass.

## Gait

In keeping with the dalmatian's historical use as a coach dog, gait and endurance are of great importance. Movement is steady and effortless. Balanced angulation fore and aft combined with powerful muscles and good condition produce smooth, efficient action. There is a powerful drive from the rear coordinated with extended reach in the front. The topline remains level. Elbows, hocks and feet turn neither in nor out. As the speed of the trot increases, there is a tendency to single track.

## Temperament

Temperament is stable and outgoing, yet dignified. Shyness is a major fault.

### Scale of Points

| | |
|---|---:|
| General Appearance | 5 |
| Size, proportion, substance | 10 |
| Head | 10 |
| Neck, topline, body | 10 |
| Forequarters | 5 |
| Hindquarters | 5 |
| Feet | 5 |
| Coat | 5 |
| Color and markings | 25 |
| Gait | 10 |
| Temperament | 10 |
| Total | 100 |

## The American Kennel Club

The American Kennel Club, established in 1884, is a nonprofit organization comprised of almost 400 dog clubs throughout the United States. Its primary purpose is to foster and maintain interest in the health and welfare of purebred dogs.

## Registering Your Dog

You must give your dog an unusual name consisting of no more than 25 letters. Names are based on heritage, markings and whimsy. Many serious breeders preface their dogs' names with a registered kennel name.

One of the AKC's responsibilities is to keep a stud book. This record contains the ancestral pedigree of every dog that has ever been registered.

## What Does a Pedigree Mean?

Your dog's pedigree is its family tree. Compiled from AKC stud book records, a pedigree proves that for generations all of the dog's ancestors were of the same breed. In addition, a pedigree contains birth dates, coat colors, and any championships and obedience titles. Some of the abbreviations on your dalmatian's pedigree might be CH (Champion), FCH (Field Champion), CD (Companion Dog), and CDX (Companion Dog Excellent.) For dog owners interested in breeding, a pedigree is essential. With this knowledge, a breeder can predict with greater accuracy such critical variables as appearance, temperament, and conformation.

## How To Read a Pedigree

The word pedigree derives from the French words for crane's foot, *pied de grue*. That is because some inspired searcher felt that the lines on a pedigree chart resembled bird tracks.

In the chart, the sire's (father's) name appears above the dam's (mother's) name in each generation.

The two-letter prefix followed by a six-digit number is your dog's registration number. The date next to this number is the month and year the dog's name was published in the AKC's stud book register.

## Where To Obtain a Copy

Once you receive your dalmatian's registration certificate, you may request its pedigree from the American Kennel Club. A three-generation pedigree will list 14 ancestors. A four-generation pedigree will list 30 ancestors.

Write to the American Kennel Club, Certified Pedigrees, 51 Madison Ave., New York, New York 10010. Include your dog's name, its AKC registration number, and its breed (dalmatian). If you want to know if the ancestors were black or liver colored, indicate this in your letter.

## The Dalmatian Club of America

The Dalmatian Club of America (DCA) is the parent organization of 30 or more active regional clubs representing over one thousand members.

The DCA holds an annual, well-attended, National Specialty Show. A quarterly publication, *The Spotter*, contains informative articles on breeders, shows, matches, training, and other useful perspectives. Applicants for membership in the DCA must be eighteen years of age or older, must own or co-own a registered dalmatian, and must be sponsored by two club members in good standing.

For further information about dalmatians and the DCA, contact the American Kennel Club.

## Showing Your Dalmatian

Many dalmatian owners are more than satisfied to have the quiet, solitary friendship of a loving, companionable dog. Together, the pair enjoy the peaceful camaraderie of quiet winter walks and boisterous autumn afternoons.

Some dogs and some owners, though, enjoy the show ring. Some dalmatians are natural showmen. Paired with an owner-handler who enjoys the show ring, the duo trot easily and well through the show routines.

Attend several shows before you decide to try your hand. Watch the dogs and the handlers. Then talk to one or two who impressed you with their love of the breed, and make arrangements for further instruction.

Why did you select a dalmatian instead of some other breed? Never mind, there is no need to answer that question. I have a mental picture of a spotted little puppy, all eyes and tail and heart, begging you to take it home. No, there's no question about why you selected a dalmatian. You fell in love.

Congratulations, and a long and happy friendship to you both!

# Useful Addresses and Literature

## Dogs In General

American Kennel Club
51 Madison Avenue
New York, New York 10010
Reference library, informational booklets,
monthly magazine, videos, and films.

Alderton, David. *The Dog Care Manual*.
Barron's Educational Series, Hauppauge,
New York, 1984.
Baer, Ted. *Communicating with Your Dog*.
Barron's Educational Series, Hauppauge,
New York, 1989.
Frye, Frederic L. *First Aid for Your Dog*.
Barron's Educational Series, Hauppauge,
New York, 1987.
Klever, Ulrich. *The Complete Book of Dog Care*.
Barron's Educational Series, Hauppauge,
New York, 1989.

Rutherford, Clarice and Neil, David H.
*How to Raise a Puppy You Can Live With*.
Alpine Publications, Colorado, 1981.
Vine, Louis, L., D.V.M. *Your Dog, His Health and Happiness*. Prentice Hall, 1986.
Whitney, Leon. D.V.M., Whitney, George,
D.V.M. *The Complete Book of Dog Care*.
Doubleday, New York, 1984.
Wolters, Richard A. *Home Dog*.
Dutton, New York, 1984.
Woodhouse, Barbara. *No Bad Dogs*.
Summit Books, New York, 1982.

## Dalmatians in Particular

Dalmatian Club of America, Inc.
Mrs. Irving Fleming, Secretary
4390 Chickasaw Road
Memphis, Tennessee 38117

# *Index*

# Index

# *Index*

# *Index*